MUSLIM INTELLECTUAL

A STUDY OF AL-GHAZALI

W. Montgomery Watt
Reader in Arabic, University of Edinburgh

ABC International Group

W. Montgomery Watt
Ḥujjat al-Islām Abū Ḥāmid Muḥammad Ghazzālī Ṭūsī
(AH450/CE1059 to AH505/CE1111), commonly known as al-Ghazzali.
The Muslim Intellectual

1. Islamic philosophy. 2. Islamic history. 3. Islamic theology—Early works to 1800. 4. Ghazzali, 1058-1111. I. Title.

ISBN: 1-57644-717-1 pbk

The cover photograph is a photograph of the tomb of al-Ghazali in northwestern Iran in a city outside of Mashhad called Tus.

Published by
ABC International Group

Distributed by
KAZI Publications, Inc.
3023 W. Belmont Avenue
Chicago IL 60618
Tel: 773-267-7001; FAX: 773-267-7002
email: info@kazi.org /www.kazi.org

CONTENTS

PREFACE

THE difficulty of writing about al-Ghazālī is well illustrated by the various comments and criticisms that have been made of the works by Julius Obermann, A. J. Wensinck, Margaret Smith and Farid Jabre. The difficulty is due to the great volume of his writings, to the fact that books were ascribed to him that were definitely not by him, and to the changes in his outlook which occurred during the course of his life. When the growth and development of his outlook is combined with the lack of complete agreement about which works are unauthentic, scholars are presented with some peculiarly intractable problems before they can properly begin the study of al-Ghazālī's thought. Yet the subject is one that is well worth attempting. Al-Ghazālī has been acclaimed as the greatest Muslim after Muḥammad, and is certainly one of the greatest. His outlook, too, is closer than that of many Muslims to the outlook of modern Europe and America, so that he is more easily comprehensible to us. Thus there is here a great challenge to scholarship.

The present study of the struggle and achievement of al-Ghazālī does not attempt to take up that challenge in its entirety, but only to look at his life and thought as a whole within the context of the times in which he lived. I have tried to write in such a way that the book could be read by general sociologists as well as by students of Islam, but this means that Islamists will find an undue neglect of detail. In defence I would make the plea that it is necessary to look at the picture as a whole before we can see at what points further detailed study is needed. The general standpoint from which I write is that of the sociology of knowledge—a discipline which, though still in its infancy, is characteristic of our age and an expression of its spirit. Since practically nothing has been written about the Islamic world from this standpoint, I have found it necessary to re-examine and reassess much of the previous history of Islamic thought. This re-assessment had largely been made, and the relevant sections of this book written, before I began *Islamic Philosophy and Theology*.

I have to thank my eldest daughter for helping with the Index and my wife for correcting proofs as well as putting up with the vagaries of a husband wrapped up in the writing of a book.

W. MONTGOMERY WATT

Edinburgh, November 1962

I

THE FUNCTION OF THE INTELLECTUAL

THIS book arises out of a concern felt by many intellectuals. In the desperate predicament of the world in which they live can they as intellectuals make any special contribution to saving it from the destruction which threatens? It was once thought that ideas controlled the course of history, and there are many remnants of this belief; but on the whole it is now discredited. Many men, instead, tend to acknowledge the dominion of economic and material factors, whether regretfully or eagerly. If ideas are powerless, then the intellectual, as the bearer of ideas, has no important functions.

In *Islam and the Integration of Society*[1] I tried to show that, while economic and material factors determine the setting of man's life, ideational factors direct his responses to the situations in which he found himself. Corresponding to this function of ideas in the life of society will be the function of the intellectuals as the persons primarily responsible for dealing with ideas. The present study is an attempt to show in detail what this handling of ideas amounts to, and the method is to examine the life and thought of one of the greatest intellectuals of Islamic society, al-Ghazālī.

It is convenient to speak of the intellectuals or intelligentsia as if they constituted a single class. Yet as soon as one begins to consider them closely, they appear to be manifold in their variety. There are all those concerned with the handing on of ideas to other people, whether school-teachers, university professors, journalists, broadcasters or writers of books. There are all those concerned with the application of ideas to detailed situations; almost everyone does this to some extent, but we might think here specially of politicians and civil servants. Even when, setting aside the transmission and application of ideas, we confine ourselves to the creative handling of ideas, there would still appear to be three aspects: instrumental, systematizing and intuitive.

(*a*) The instrumental intellectual *par excellence* is the scientist, who investigates our environment and thereby increases our control over it. Even the pure scientist, who does not think of the practical applications of his work, is in fact performing this function for his society. At the present time men are developing the social sciences, and thereby increasing the possibilities of controlling society and other men. (*b*) Representatives of the systematizing trend are the philosopher, the philosophically-minded scientist, the theologian, the legal theorist, and perhaps the historian where he is finding general rules implicit in particular events. (*c*) The intuitive intellectual may be said to be concerned with the values acknowledged in a society and their basis in reality. A prophetic leader like Muḥammad, who directed far-reaching social and political movements, is a good example of the intuitive intellectual. But in the same group would also come poets and other litterateurs, and likewise historians and humanistic scholars. The politician is placed here in so far as he is dealing with lofty and important issues.[2]

While these three aspects are clearly distinct, they are probably seldom found in their pure state. Systematization is usually a type of activity that does not proceed automatically but requires an element of intuition. There may even be an element of intuition lurking in the results of the scientist, especially of the social scientist. The present study is chiefly concerned with the ideas which are fundamental to the whole life of Islamic society, and these belong primarily to the intuitive aspect. Because of the intermingling of the aspects in actual life, however, it will not be necessary to label particular men as intuitives or systematizers. It is also to be noted that in so far as the response to a situation is intuitive it is partly unconscious; the intellectual need not be fully aware either of that to which he is responding or of the precise manner of his response to it.

The phrase "bearers of ideas" suggests a measure of passivity, but the intuitive intellectual is essentially creative. Such creativity cannot be avoided. A society is a living thing, and the situation to which it has to respond is constantly changing. Even where the economic and material framework of its life is stable, there is a constant movement of social adjustment which goes to constitute the given situation at any time. The ideational basis of a relatively stable society has a certain fixity, but it is also always undergoing modification in detail, even if only in respect of emphasis. This modification is the work of the intuitive intellectual. Ideas, too, even when they remain ostensibly unchanged, may through material and social changes come to fulfil a different role in the life of society. The outstanding case of this is where ideas, which were originally sound and appropriate to the time, become ideological (in the technical sense) through being used to bolster up a sectional privilege which in the interests of society as a whole ought to be abolished. An example in the field of religion is the case of the Pharisees in the New Testament. Their ideas were substantially the same as those of the religious leaders of the Jews some two hundred years earlier. In the earlier period the ideas were an appropriate bastion for the defence of the Jewish religion against the cultural attack of Hellenism; but in the later period they had become a vehicle for the self-satisfied pride, complacency and even hypocrisy which we now associate with Pharisaism.

It is not necessary here to try to classify all the types of adaptation that are required of intellectuals, but only to notice that there are several different types. In so far as the society is a homogeneous one, the main types of adaptation will be to changed material circumstances and to the changed social conditions arising out of the material changes. The adaptation consists in the modification of the ideational basis of the society so that activity in accordance with the new ideational basis is a more satisfactory response to the existing situation. A society such as that of the Islamic world, however, is not homogeneous. Besides the different social classes there are—often cutting across class divisions—groups from divergent cultural backgrounds. Here part of the work of the intellectual is to attempt to find an ideational synthesis which will increase the integration in the society and decrease the tensions. Ideally such an ideational synthesis is a complex of ideas in which each group can find those elements in which it is chiefly interested, and find them in a form which does not offend other groups. The intellectual can only achieve this modification and adaptation in so far as he is himself involved in his society and its tensions. Sometimes he can deliberately bring about such involvement—as al-Ghazālī did when he set about studying the views of the philosophers and the Bāṭinites and genuinely trying to appreciate the truth in them. Where there is tension between two sections of a society, there is a place for intellectuals in each section; but the most satisfying and lasting work for an intellectual would appear to be in maintaining a certain detachment from the contending factions.

A study such as the present cannot be completely objective, since the writer's own attitude to religion enters into his assessment and presentation of the facts. The best way to minimize the harmful effects of this subjective bias is to try to make explicit what one's attitude is.

So far as I am aware, then, the following three points define the attitude to religion on which this investigation is based:

(1) Human life has significance, meaning or transcendent value. The word "transcendent" here indicates that this value is not negated by death or transiency, not even by the disappearance of human life from the solar system.

(2) This transcendent value is normally given what may be called an "ontological basis". That is, it is demonstrated, or perhaps merely asserted, that reality is such that the value is indeed transcendent; for example, Marxists assert that the dialectic of history inevitably leads to the classless society. Whether this "ontological basis" is true or false, and whether it is meaningful here to speak about truth and falsehood, are questions belonging to another discipline. All that is assumed in this study is that the "ontological basis" is a set of ideas which has sociological functions. It might be said, of course, that such an assumption implies that the "ontological basis" has a degree or measure of truth.

(3) The language in which the transcendent value and the "ontological basis" are expressed is closer to that of poetry than to that of science. In pointing or hinting at the nature of reality it is necessarily vaguer than language based on sense-experience. This makes it possible for different religions and sects to refer to the same (or almost the same) aspect of reality in ways that are superficially contradictory. (The extent to which such contradictions are based on "pre-religious" categories of thinking is a subject requiring further investigation.)

II
THE WORLD OF AL-GHAZĀLĪ

I THE POLITICAL BACKGROUND

In a sense the background of the life of any individual is the whole previous history of his civilization. For an understanding of al-Ghazālī it will be sufficient to glance briefly at the history of the Islamic empire or caliphate from the death of Muḥammad in 632 to the birth of al-Ghazālī in 1058. In these four centuries four main phases may be distinguished, which may be labelled: conquests; conversion; disintegration; reconstitution. These phases follow one another chronologically, but overlap to some extent.

(1) *The Conquests.* As Muḥammad lay on his deathbed in Medina an expedition was being assembled on the outskirts of the town whose task was in fact to open the way for the conquest of Syria. For the next two years, however, the Muslim leaders were busy suppressing revolts in Arabia, but in the following ten years the small state with its centre at Medina wrested the rich provinces of Syria and Egypt from the Byzantine empire and that of Iraq from the Persian empire, besides sending the latter reeling to destruction. A hundred years after Muḥammad's death the sway of his successor extended from north of the Pyrenees, through North Africa and the Fertile Crescent to Central Asia (Transoxiana) and the Punjab.

The effective control of these vast territories after the amazingly rapid conquest was made possible by the simplicity of the central organization. The Arabs constituted themselves into a vast army. At the extremities of their domains they had the help of auxiliaries from such peoples as the Berbers, but otherwise the army of Arabs did all the fighting and all the garrison-work. The local administrations were taken over and continued to function much as before. All that the Arab provincial governors had to do was to have direct supervision over the army and then to see that the non-Arab local administration was effective and handed over the due taxes.

The head of this state was called the caliph or successor (*sc.* of Muḥammad), and had inherited the latter's administrative but not his prophetic functions; the state is correspondingly known as the caliphate. From the description given it will be seen that it is essentially an Arab-Muslim military aristocracy; or rather, only those who are Arabs and Muslims are full citizens, serving in the army and in return drawing an annual stipend. The non-Muslims were related to the Muslim government not as individuals but as groups, later known as millets, and usually with a religious basis; e.g. the Christians of Jerusalem or the Jews of Iraq. Such a group had internal autonomy under its religious head, who was responsible to the government for handing over the taxes. Since it was a matter of honour for the ruler to make the official protection of such groups effective, there was practically no religious persecution. Yet the suggestion that these "protected persons" were second-class citizens meant that there was a constant pressure on them to become Muslims. On the whole the system has worked well and made life tolerable for millions; but it has tended to "freeze" small groups and prevent their assimilation in the larger whole except at a very slow rate (by conversions to Islam). The present troubles with minorities in the Middle East are largely due to the breakdown of the millet system of the Ottoman empire.

(2) *Conversion*. Islam was by tradition a missionary

religion, and was, at least implicitly, of universal validity. Because of its Arabic origin, however, there was a tendency to think of it as primarily for Arabs. This tendency was reinforced during the first century of the caliphate by the desire of the Arab Muslims to retain their privileged position as first-class citizens. Little effort was made in the early decades to convert non-Arabs to Islam. When non-Arabs insisted on becoming Muslims, whatever their motives may have been, they had to be attached to Arab tribes as "clients". This still had a suggestion of inferiority. As the number of non-Arab Muslims increased, their discontent with their status and demand for equality was one of the factors behind the movement which replaced the Umayyad caliphs of Damascus (who had ruled from 660 to 750) by the 'Abbāsid caliphs of Baghdad. This change was not simply a change of dynasty; it was a change of the basis of the caliphate. The body politic was now more explicitly based on Islamic principles and regarded as a "charismatic community";[1] and all Muslims, whether Arab or not, were full citizens. The establishment of the 'Abbāsid caliphate thus reflected the fact that many non-Arabs had been converted to Islam.

Yet the change of dynasty also meant in various ways a return to Persian ideas of autocratic government. Under the Umayyads power had been shared between the new Islamic aristocracy (who received higher stipends because they or their ancestors had become Muslims at an early date) and sections of the old Arab aristocracy. At many points actions had been based on traditional Arab political ideas, derived from experience with tribes and confederations of tribes; but in several ways this was unsatisfactory, and unsuited for a vast empire. Under the earlier 'Abbāsids power was almost exclusively in the hands of the caliph and his court. Since membership of the court was virtually in the gift of the caliph, this meant that power was in the hands of the caliph and one or two other men, such as the Barmakid viziers; how far the caliph had to share his power depended on his strength and capacity for controlling affairs. Within the court circle, that is, within the ruling institution, there was practically no check on the autocratic decisions of the caliph; and contemporary chronicles depict a naked struggle for power in which nothing was barred. On the other hand, the relations between the ruling institution and those ruled were largely determined by Islamic principles as stated in the Sharī'a or revealed law. The general acceptance of Islamic principles outside the court circle produced during the next century or two a high degree of homogeneity in the vast and varied empire.

(3) *Disintegration.* After the first enthusiasm had waned the 'Abbāsids found it increasingly difficult to exercise effective control over their domains. Provincial governors had to be given large powers, including the command of considerable armies. If they disliked some order from the caliph, they could hardly be forced to obey it. They tended to present the caliph with a series of *faits accomplis*, such as the extension of the boundaries of their province, which he was obliged to ratify. At length demands came that a son should succeed to the governorship, and the caliph had to accede. Thus there came into being local dynasties, for all practical purposes autonomous, but making a formal acknowledgement of the supremacy of the caliph. This description is specially applicable to the east, where there are four dynasties which deserve to be mentioned.

(*a*) Ṭāhirids. Five men (four generations) of the Ṭāhirid family maintained themselves as governors of Khurāsān from 820 to 872. From the standpoint of the present study it is worth noting that the Ṭāhirids, by making Nishapur their capital, gave a fillip to its development as an intellectual and cultural centre. Their downfall resulted not from any action of the caliph but from military defeat by the first of the Ṣaffārids.

(*b*) Ṣaffārids. Three men of the Ṣaffārid family, starting shortly before 868 from the governorship of Sijistān (roughly southern Afghanistan), extended their rule (by 872) to most of southern and eastern Persia up to the Oxus, and maintained themselves there until about 903.

(*c*) Samānids. The Samānid family is reckoned as having ruled from 874 to 999, and has a complex history which need not be described here. The chief basis of their power was Transoxiana, and their eastern capital, Bukhārā, became a literary and cultural centre of great brilliance.[2] After they had wrested Khurāsān from the Ṣaffārids (900–910) Nishapur became their second capital, not far behind Bukhārā in the splendour of its intellectual life.

(*d*) Ghaznavids. The Ghaznavid dynasty (976–1186) was of Turkish race, being descended from officers in the Samānid armies. Subuktigīn became governor in the mountain town of Ghazna (about a hundred miles south of Kābul in Afghanistan), and extended his power both towards India and into eastern Persia. His son, Maḥmūd of Ghazna (*regnabat* 998–1030), repudiated Samānid suzerainty, was appointed governor of Khurāsān and Ghazna directly by the caliph, and made great conquests in India. Soon after the death of Maḥmūd, however, the dynasty began to be deprived by the Seljūqs of its domains in Persia and Transoxiana, so that from about 1050 its rule was restricted to Afghanistan and India.

Further west there were small dynasties which developed from provincial governorships and continued to acknowledge the caliph of Baghdad. In the west, however, there were also actual losses of territory. A few years after the overthrow of the Umayyad caliph by the ʿAbbāsids, a member of the Umayyad family became independent ruler of Spain, though without claiming to be caliph. Such a claim was first made by the Fāṭimids, a dynasty which established itself first in Tunisia in 909, and then in 969 transferred the seat of its power to Egypt. The Fāṭimid rulers claimed to be the rightful caliphs of the whole Islamic world, and sent emissaries into the ʿAbbāsid domains to preach revolution. No more need be said about the Fāṭimids here, since their propaganda (also known as Ismāʿīlite or Bāṭinite) became a major concern for al-Ghazālī (chapter IV).

(4) *Reconstitution.* The word "reconstitution" is not altogether satisfactory as a description of the fourth phase of the caliphate, but it is convenient to have a single word. In this phase the caliph loses most of his remaining power, though he retains his position as a figurehead with certain official functions and dignities. Real power passed into the hands of a series of war-lords, who eventually came to have the title of "sultan". The first of these war-lords was Ibn-Rā'iq, who entered Baghdad at the head of an army in 936 and simply took over the machinery of government from the caliph's vizier. As a Muslim historian puts it: [3]

"From this time the power of the viziers ceased. The vizier no longer had control of the provinces, the bureaux or the departments; he had merely the title of vizier, and the right of appearing on ceremonial days at the Palace in black with sword and belt."

Ibn-Rā'iq held this lofty position for less than two years, but in 945 Baghdad was captured by the Buwayhid (or Būyid) family—chiefs of a warlike highland tribe from Daylam, at the south of the Caspian Sea—who assumed the reins of government, and held them, though latterly with a slackening grip, until 1055. Their direct rule extended over Iraq and a large part of Persia, but provinces were entrusted to different members of the family, and these did not always see eye to eye.

The Buwayhids eventually fell before another family of war-lords, the Seljūqs, who, supported by Turkish tribesmen, first made themselves masters of Khurāsān, and then in 1055 established themselves in Baghdad. At its widest extent their empire was much greater than that of the Buwayhids, including Syria in the west and Transoxiana and the whole of Persia in the east. This was the situation during the maturity of al-Ghazālī, but before his death in 1111 the central government was weakening and it eventually disintegrated in 1157. This is as far as we need follow the history of the caliphate.

This phase of reconstitution has various aspects. While in one way it was the end of the rule of the caliphs, in another way it was a restoration to the central government of the territories directly under the caliph. In this new central government the place of military power was more explicit. The early conquests had been made by a citizen army, but in course of time a citizen army was shown to have disadvantages. In any case, after conversion became frequent there were too many citizens for the army. In practice it was found more satisfactory to have mercenaries, though this meant that the officers of the mercenaries might have undue power. It was becoming clear that political power depended on military backing. Those who were successful in the struggle for power, like the Buwayhids and the Seljūqs, were groups of men—not isolated individuals—who had effective military support that was in part independent of monetary payments. Political power partly also depended on the acquiescence of the citizens, and this was gained by recognition of the Islamic basis of society—acknowledgement of the caliph, participation in worship on certain occasions, continuation of courts applying the Sharīʿa. In major political decisions, however, and in the functioning of the court Islamic principles counted for nothing.

Despite this apparently unsatisfactory state of affairs (at least from a theoretical standpoint), the earlier part of the Seljūq period, especially the reigns of Alp-Arslān (1063–72) and Malik-Shāh (1072–92), was a time of comparative peace and prosperity and of great cultural achievement.[4] To this happy condition the wise and efficient vizier of these two sultans, Niẓām-al-Mulk, made an outstanding contribution. Though nominally subordinate to the sultan, he was practically all-powerful during these thirty years.

2 THE RELIGIOUS AND INTELLECTUAL BACKGROUND

The religion of Islam in its earlier forms was adapted to the social and intellectual needs of Mecca, Medina and Arabia.[5] But the framework of material circumstances in which it had to function even under the Umayyad caliphs was entirely different from that of Muḥammad's closing years.

The first phase of development, the conquests, quite apart from the effects on the subject peoples, involved a vast social upheaval for the Arabs, that is, the Muslims. The old tribal and clan system broke down; and, since it was through the tribe that a man's life became meaningful, this led to a religious as well as a social crisis. An important section of the Arabs dealt with this crisis by substituting for the tribe the Islamic community. Life became meaningful for them through membership of this community, since it was divinely founded and was living in accordance with divinely-given mores. But the question of how to deal with those who transgressed God's commands proved intractable, and there was much bitter argument before it was solved. In the end, however, a way was found by which the whole community, despite the presence of sinners in it, could be regarded as a "saving sect", so that membership led to everlasting bliss.[6]

The phase of "conversion" was a piece of social adjustment following on the incorporation of vast territories and their inhabitants in the Islamic empire. While some material self-interest may have been a factor in conversion, the major factor was perhaps the religious one—the attractiveness of the dynamic image of the Islamic community as a charismatic one. Men felt they wanted really to belong to this, not just to be loosely attached to it. The conception of the Islamic community as charismatic, originally developed for Arab tribesmen whose tribe had broken down, was further developed by the non-Arab Muslims. The distinctive excellences of the community, especially its possession in the Sharīʿa of a divinely-revealed law or rather set of practices, were linked with its charismatic nature. Zeal for the charismatic community was an important factor behind the incredible intellectual efforts expended in the elaboration of the Sharīʿa.

In the course of elaborating the Sharīʿa something else was also done. Many of the new converts came from a higher cultural level than the Arabs, and naturally retained most of their culture. The pious scholars in whose hands the Sharīʿa took shape not merely developed the principles found in the Qur'ān by adding to them the Traditions, that is, anecdotes about Muḥammad's words and practices. Somehow or other, almost without any conscious deception, these scholars managed to include among the Traditions much of the inherited wisdom of the Middle East, transmitted through Christian, Jewish, Gnostic and other sources. To the modern student this is all the more remarkable since Muslims had a complex system of criticism of Traditions. Careful examination, however, shows that this system was not aimed at ascertaining objective historical fact, but at excluding the views of the eccentrics or "lunatic fringe"; and this it largely succeeded in doing. The effect of systematic criticism was in fact to stabilize the Islamic religion on a new ideational basis, namely, that amalgam of Qur'ānic principle, early practice and older lore which had come to be accepted by the main body of Muslims round about the year 800. This amalgam, it is to be noted, did not include the higher learning of the Middle East, such as Greek philosophy and science; and the correct attitude to these " foreign " sciences is one of the problems which al-Ghazālī had to tackle.

By these ideational developments the religion of Islam adapted itself with considerable adequacy to the changes of the first two phases of conquest and conversion. The point where its adaptation had been least adequate was *within* the ruling institution. There Persian traditions of autocracy and the unprincipled use of power had become dominant, even though in the relations of the rulers to the ruled Islamic principles continued to be respected. In the succeeding phases this impotence of Islamic principles in the topmost political levels—so curious in view of Islam's reputation in Europe of being a political religion[7]—contributed to the difficulties of the intellectual class, and so to the major problem al-Ghazālī had to solve.

It would be convenient to describe with similar brevity the religious and ideational repercussions of the third and fourth historical stages (of disintegration and reconstitution); but unfortunately it is not possible. These repercussions have not yet been properly investigated from the standpoint of this study. Moreover, their investigation cannot be altogether separated from the problem of al-Ghazālī himself. As our understanding of this great man increases, we get more light on what had been happening in the two centuries or so before his birth. The economic, political, social, intellectual and religious happenings of these centuries made the setting in which his life had to be lived. It is part of the aim of this study to discover the salient features of that setting and what had most contributed to making them what they were. At this preliminary stage in the investigation three points may be noted.

(*a*) The standard Islamic ideational system had taken root nearly everywhere. The war-lords were under the necessity of recognizing it publicly in all their dealings with the populace. Consequently the disintegration of the caliphate under the war-lords led not to a diminution of Islamic intellectual culture but to its encouragement in numerous local centres. Among the most vigorous of these centres was Nishapur and the surrounding region, where al-Ghazālī's early life was spent.

(*b*) In the fourth phase, and also in the third phase though less obviously, supreme rule belonged to superior military force. This happened in a community which had hitherto been regarded as charismatic or divinely-constituted. Did it mean that the community lost its charismatic nature? Was the difficulty a serious one for the men of the time?

(*c*) Al-Ghazālī's abandonment of the standard career of a religious intellectual or scholar-jurist[8] suggests that there was something wrong with this career. Was it that it implied subservience to godless rulers? Were the intellectuals trying to find the significance of their lives in a framework in which Islam was irrelevant? Was the difficulty that the Sharīʿa, whose ostensible purpose was to direct the affairs of the body politic, obviously did not do this?

Al-Ghazālī himself in his autobiography speaks of four groups of men who were trying to find an adequate response to the situation, and we can do no better than follow his guidance and investigate the attitudes of these four groups: the philosophers; the Bāṭinites or Ismāʿīlites; the theologians (among whom we may make a further distinction between Ashʿarites and Ḥanbalites); the ṣūfīs or mystics.

It remains to say a word about a fifth possible response to the situation, a response in which al-Ghazālī might have been interested but in fact was not—the Persian renascence. Before the Arab conquest of Persia the Zoroastrian clergy, to preserve their power as an intellectual class, had become closely allied with the rulers and subservient to them. In so doing they had largely become cut off from the ordinary people. When the phase of conversion began, therefore, it was not surprising that many Persians became Muslims. The Persian Muslims had much to do with the establishing of the ʿAbbāsid dynasty, and in return the equality of all Muslims, Arab and non-Arab, came to be generally recognized. After a time there was a movement among the secretary class or civil service which maintained the inferiority of the Arabs; but this Shuʿūbite movement, as it was called, was chiefly a literary movement, it would seem, without much political influence. Other forms of Persian self-assertion are connected with Manichaeanism and with certain sects of Shīʿite Islam.[9]

The real awakening of the Persian spirit, however, did not come until after the phase of disintegration. Local or provincial dynasties, especially the Samānids, were a focus for hopes and aspirations. It should not be supposed, of course, that there already was a Persian nationalism comparable to the nationalisms of the nineteenth century. There was potentially something similar to these nationalisms, but it had to become conscious of itself. The chief part in bringing about this national self-awareness was played by Firdawsī (d. 1020–1025). His great epic, the *Shāh-nāma*, welded many local traditions into a unity and gave men of Persian descent a renewed enthusiasm for the perennial mission of Iran—defence of civilization from the inroads of Turan, the Turkish "barbarians" from the great steppes. This was a mission which could be combined with membership of the Islamic empire, though one imagines that the Persians would have found it difficult to go on for centuries serving these two masters, Persian secular aggrandizement and the extension of Islam.

In favourable circumstances this Persian movement might have grown and become of much political significance. Circumstances were against it, however. Before Firdawsī had completed his great poem the sun of the Samānids was setting, and in the ascendant was the star of a Muslim Turkish general, Maḥmūd of Ghazna. Indeed, Maḥmūd became Firdawsī's patron, though it is not surprising in view of his Turkish origin that he and the poet fell out.[10] He was soon followed by the Seljūqs, more Muslim Turks. With Persia largely under Turkish rule Firdawsī's conception of the roles of Iran and Turan had become no more than a political mirage. Persians had become weaker politically, and in their place Turks were now the military defenders of Muslim civilization. This was the position from a few years before al-Ghazālī's birth, and it is thus understandable that, though he must have had much Persian blood in his veins, he never seems to have been attracted by a "Persian" solution of current problems or even to have shown special interest in things Persian.[10a]

3 AL-GHAZĀLĪ'S EARLY LIFE

The central figure of this study was born in 1058, four and a half centuries after the migration of Muḥammad from Mecca to Medina, and three years after the establishment of Seljūq rule in Baghdad. His birth-place was the town or district of Ṭūs, near the modern Meshed in north-east Persia. His name was Muḥammad, and he was son of Muḥammad, son of Muḥammad; he had the honorific title (*kunya*) of Abū-Ḥāmid, meaning father of Ḥāmid but not necessarily implying that he had a son of this name (certainly only daughters survived him). He is best known as al-Ghazālī, the Ghazālite, possibly meaning the man from Ghazāla, an otherwise unknown village in the region of Ṭūs;[11] he is sometimes also called aṭ-Ṭūsī, the Ṭūsite. He had one brother, Aḥmad, who became a distinguished scholar and mystic, and several sisters.

Nothing is known for certain about his family except that he had a grand-uncle (or less probably uncle), also called Abū-Ḥāmid al-Ghazālī, who was one of the scholars of Ṭūs and died about 1043. The family was thus in touch with intellectual circles, as is also shown by the father's anxiety that his two sons should receive the fullest possible education. The assertion in some sources that the theologian's father was a spinner and vendor of wool is to be rejected, since it appears to be an inference from the less probable spelling and derivation of the name Ghazālī. It may be accepted, however, that the father was comparatively poor. On his death he left as much money as he could with a ṣūfī friend, charging him to see that the two boys were well educated. When the money was exhausted the friend made arrangements for them to go to a college or *madrasa* where they could receive free board and lodging as well as instruction. This very brief glimpse of al-Ghazālī's family shows that the family background was not without its influence on his later career. His father would be characterized by the simple piety of ordinary Muslims, based no doubt on a considerable knowledge of the Qur'ān and the Traditions which could be gained by attendance at the lectures given freely in the mosques. Towards the end of his life al-Ghazālī wrote a book in which he advocated prohibiting ordinary people from attending lectures on theology,[12] but this must be taken to apply only to the abstruse rational theology of the time and not to the more concrete forms of religious instruction.

No dates are recorded for the earlier part of al-Ghazālī's education. The normal age to begin schooling was eleven, and he would be eleven in 1069.[13] In 1077 he went to an important school or college at Nishapur, the capital of this part of Persia, to study under the most distinguished theologian of the age, al-Juwaynī.[14] In the intervening years he pursued his studies mainly at Ṭūs, apart from a visit to Gurgan (Jurjān) at the south-east corner of the Caspian Sea. (Nishapur is about fifty miles from Ṭūs, Gurgan over three hundred, the road passing through Nishapur; these were comparatively short journeys for a great scholar.)[15] The story is told of how the caravan in which the young student was travelling back from Gurgan was set upon by robbers. Among the goods they seized were the notebooks, with the harvest of his study in Gurgan. He went after the robbers and pled for the return of his notebooks, which contained, as he phrased it, the knowledge he had gained at Gurgan. The robber-chief scoffed at this alleged knowledge which could be taken away so easily, but gave back the notebooks. The visit to Gurgan cannot have been later than 1074, since al-Ghazālī on his return spent three years committing his "knowledge" to memory.

In these years of study at Ṭūs, Gurgan and Nishapur, al-Ghazālī followed the standard curriculum of Islamic higher education. This had a predominantly legal slant. The basis was the study of the Qur'ān and Traditions, together with the commentaries on these. Jurisprudence was derived mainly from the Traditions. Then there were ancillary sciences such as Arabic grammar, differences between the recognized legal rites, and biographical knowledge of the transmitters of Traditions. In al-Ghazālī's case, at least until he went to Nishapur, the chief emphasis was on Traditions and jurisprudence. In these subjects the standard of instruction in Ṭūs and Gurgan may well have been high. For over a century Nishapur and the neighbouring regions had been in the forefront of educational development, doubtless owing to the virtual independence of the Samānids and their patronage of learning and the arts.

Instruction in the "Islamic sciences" had originally been given in mosques without any fees, and this practice continued. Gradually, however, special institutions were created. At first they may have consisted merely of a room or hall and a library. In course of time living-quarters for the students were added, and funds made available for their support. To this latter form of institution the name *madrasa* is given, which may be rendered "college". The first such college seems to have been founded in Nishapur before 960, and this was followed within the century by several others. The movement of college-founding was vigorously encouraged by Niẓām-al-Mulk, the great Seljūq vizier (in power from 1063 to 1092). One source suggests that he was the first to provide "scholarships" for the students; but some earlier cases are known.[16] What is certain is that he founded at least nine Niẓāmiyya colleges, scattered from Mosul to Herat, and that they were lavishly endowed. In 1077 Nishapur had enjoyed relative peace under the Seljūqs for nearly forty years, whereas Baghdad had been the scene of strife, which must have made academic work difficult, till after the Seljūq occupation in 1055. It might, therefore, be expected that the level of academic attainment in the region of Nishapur would be among the highest in the Islamic world.

In particular, when al-Ghazālī went to Nishapur in 1077 it was to the Niẓāmiyya college he went, attracted by the fame of the great theologian, Abū-'l-Maʿālī al-Juwaynī, known as Imām-al-Ḥaramayn, "the imam of the two holy places" (Mecca and Medina). Al-Juwaynī was the son of a professor or lecturer at Nishapur, but was admitted by all to be more brilliant than his father. He was primarily a theologian, and introduced al-Ghazālī to theology, perhaps the most difficult of the Islamic sciences. Al-Ghazālī remained at Nishapur until al-Juwaynī's death in August 1085, and latterly helped with teaching. Then he went to the camp of Niẓām-al-Mulk, and was received by the vizier with honour and respect, though still only twenty-seven. Though one would have expected him to go on teaching in Nishapur, the records suggest that he spent the whole of the next few years at the camp, until his appointment as professor at the Niẓāmiyya college in Baghdad in July 1091.[17]

Thus we see that al-Ghazālī had an education as good as any to be had in the Islamic world. Al-Juwaynī was the first theologian of his time. His teachers in Tradition were not so eminent, but his inexactitude in quoting Traditions and his use of uncanonical Traditions are probably due mainly to his own slackness and unorthodoxy. Education, too, had struck deep roots in the region round Nishapur and Ṭūs, and had influenced many classes of society. This meant that al-Ghazālī, while gaining an excellent education, was not cut off from the simple but well-informed faith of the ordinary people. Al-Ju-waynī is reported to have made a statement which indicates how the younger man was moulded by the older in this point and in others:[18]

"I heard Abū-'l-Maʿālī al-Juwaynī saying, I had read thousands of books; then I left the people of Islam with their religion and their manifest sciences in these books, and I embarked on the open sea, plunging into the literature the people of Islam rejected. All this was in quest of truth. At an early age I fled from the acceptance of others' opinions (*taqlīd*). But now I have returned from everything to the word of the Truth, 'Hold to the religion of the old women'. If the Truth does not grasp me by the grace of His justice, so that I die in the religion of the old women and the result of my life is sealed at my departure with the purity of the people of Truth and the word of sincerity, 'There is no god but God', then alas for the son of al-Juwaynī (that is, himself)."

III

THE ENCOUNTER WITH PHILOSOPHY

1 THE PHILOSOPHICAL MOVEMENT IN THE ISLAMIC WORLD

In its main outlines the story is well known of how Greek philosophy entered the Islamic world and was partly incorporated into Islamic theology, but about the details there is still much obscurity.[1] The aim of this and the following section is not to investigate some of the many remaining obscurities, but to look at the place of the philosophers in Islamic society.

It was only under the early ʿAbbāsids that Muslims began to have effective contacts with Greek learning, though within the territories ruled by the caliph this was still alive at a number of Christian colleges, notably one at Gundē-Shāpūr (or Junday-sābūr, about a hundred miles north-east of Basra). The decisive step was taken by the caliph al-Manṣūr (*regnabat* 754–775), whose health was not good, when in 765 he summoned to his court a doctor from Gundē-Shāpūr, George of the Persian-Nestorian family of Bokhtīshūʿ; until 870 the post of court physician was held by George and his descendants, and other members of the family are heard of subsequently.[2] From 765 onwards interest in all the aspects of Greek learning grew in the court circle, encouraged by such men as the Barmakid family of viziers. Noted patrons and amateurs of Greek learning were Hārūn ar-Rashīd (*regnabat* 786–809) and his son al-Ma'mūn (813–833). Under the three caliphs mentioned and their immediate successors a beginning was made with the work of translating Greek books into Arabic (usually from the Syriac translations already possessed by the Christian colleges), and a few bold spirits would attempt to combine Greek and Islamic ideas.

Three main stages may be distinguished in the work of translation. The first is that already described. To begin with, the patronage was sporadic, but al-Ma'mūn gave the matter an institutional basis by setting up a "house of wisdom" (*bayt al-ḥikma*), which was both a library and a centre for the copying and translating of books. By 850 a fair number of Greek medical texts and several of the works of Aristotle and other philosophers were available in Arabic. Since an Arabic technical vocabulary in these disciplines had to be created, the achievement was considerable, even if some of the more abstruse works were still imperfectly comprehended. The second stage is that of Ḥunayn ibn-Is'ḥāq (*vivebat* 808–873) and his son and other pupils. Ḥunayn was of Arab descent, had studied grammar at Basra and medicine at Baghdad, and then travelled widely in the Byzantine empire as well as the Islamic. From his travels he brought back an excellent knowledge of Greek and a valuable collection of manuscripts. His scholarly standards in translation were of the highest; for him a necessary preliminary of translations was the construction of a critical Greek text. In general the translations of Ḥunayn and his school reached a new level of accuracy and comprehension. The third stage in the work of translation corresponds roughly to the tenth century. Owing to the development of original philosophical writing in Arabic there was a more profound understanding of the problems and a richer technical vocabulary. Some of the older translations were revised (as Ḥunayn also had done). Such fresh translations as were made, however, were from Syriac and not directly from Greek.

It was mainly out of the work of translation that the

independent philosophical movement grew in the Islamic world. In this movement there are various trends. With the attachment to the caliphal court of the family of Bokhtīshūʿ, the medical tradition of Gundē-Shāpūr began to take root in Baghdad. There was a hospital under the supervision of the court physician, and here medical teaching was given. There was probably also some instruction in philosophy; certainly all doctors of the period studied philosophy.

A second important strand was the philosophical tradition of Alexandria. The great college at Alexandria had never had very close relations with its Coptic-speaking Egyptian hinterland, being essentially a Greek institution. It is significant that Syriac had begun to replace Greek before the Arab conquest. This latter event presumably led to the withdrawal of the remaining Greek-speaking (as distinct from Syriac-speaking or Coptic-speaking) teachers. The connection with Syriac scholarship doubtless determined the selection of Antioch as a new site for the college about 718, when it had presumably become too small to continue in Egypt. Round about 850 there was another move, this time westwards to Ḥarrān (about halfway along the route to Mosul), and towards 900 yet another, to Baghdad. These moves were essentially moves of the teachers, the living bearers of the philosophical tradition, though on some occasions they are also reported as having taken the library with them. From about 850 something is known about the chief philosophers connected with this tradition. In particular there was a lively philosophical coterie meeting in the house of Abū-Sulaymān al-Manṭiqī as-Sijistānī in Baghdad in the last quarter of the tenth century.[3]

There were also other strands about which we are not so well informed. The so-called sect of Ṣābi'ans in Ḥarrān had made some study of Greek philosophy, and certain members of it became involved in the translation work and the philosophical movement in Baghdad. The college transferred from Antioch to Ḥarrān, however, seems to have been separate and under Christian direction. In the eastern parts of the caliphate there were also some philosophical studies, which made possible the appearance of a man like Muḥammad ibn-Zakarīyā ar-Rāzī. It seems likely that philosophical works were translated into Persian at Gundē-Shāpūr and elsewhere, but the suggestion that works of Aristotle were translated from Persian into Arabic has been shown to be without foundation.[4]

What of the people who were involved in this philosophical movement? Who were they, what was their position in society, and why were they interested in philosophy?

First of all there were the caliphs like al-Manṣūr and al-Ma'mūn. As they became aware of the "foreign sciences" which were being cultivated within their empire, they must have wanted to gain what practical benefits were to be had from them. Medical treatment had obvious advantages, and so doctors are found to have played a large part in the philosophical movement. Astrology was also assigned a high practical importance, and the contemporary amalgam of astrology and astronomy was much cultivated. Mathematics, too, had its practical use. The same could not be said of philosophy, but it may have been included because it was closely linked with the other branches of Greek learning. In any case it was a part of this new, exciting and in some ways "higher" culture.

Al-Ma'mūn had as friends and advisers a group of Islamic theologians known as Mu'tazilites. Some of these had been involved in defending Islam by argument against non-Muslims, and they soon perceived the usefulness of Greek logic and other Greek philosophical ideas in such arguments. Consequently they boldly engaged in speculation, and interpreted traditional Islamic doctrines in terms of Greek ideas to the scandal of the more conservative theologians. They will have to be discussed more fully at a later stage of this study. Here, after this brief mention, they may be left aside, since they were not philosophers but theologians who to a limited extent made use of Greek ideas.

At a later period than that of al-Ma'mūn, minor rulers in the provinces are found patronizing students of philosophy and the other Greek sciences. In some cases they may have been chiefly interested in a man's medical knowledge; but al-Fārābī, who never practised as a doctor, was well-received at the court of Sayf-ad-Dawla in Syria (about 945). In such a case it may be that the local ruler was emulating the court of the caliph; but it is also conceivable that he may have wanted to maintain a degree of independence from the scholar-jurists (though this is a point which requires further investigation).

Of the many Christians involved in the philosophical movement nothing will be said here, since their motives can only be understood in the context of the history of the relations between Christianity and philosophy. Some of the Christians gained a living as doctors, others had positions in their ecclesiastical institutions.

The point on which our attention must be focussed is the chain of Muslim philosophers and the position of each in society.

(1) The earliest of all, al-Kindī[5] (*c.* 800–866 or –873), known as "the philosopher of the Arabs", came from an Arab family which had held official posts rising to the governorship of Kūfa. He himself was attached to the caliphal court, and was tutor to a son of one of the caliphs. He had a large library, presumably mainly of books in the Greek sciences, in which he was an expert. The library was removed to Basra to inconvenience him as

the result of a court intrigue, but was subsequently restored. (2) A pupil of al-Kindī's, Aḥmad ibn-aṭ-Ṭayyib as-Sarakhsī (d. 896), had administrative and other positions at the caliph's court, including the tutorship of a future caliph, but had time to write about philosophy.[6] (3) After the transference of the former Alexandrian college from Ḥarrān to Baghdad a man called Ibn-Karnīb is said to have become head of it (shortly after 900?). His father and brother were mathematicians and wrote on astronomy, and he himself is said to have been both a theologian (*mutakallim*) and a natural-scientist. He earned his living, however, as a secretary (or civil servant).

(4) The great physician ar-Rāzī, known in Europe as Rhazes (865–923 or –932), completed his education at Baghdad, though he spent the early part of his life at Rayy (near modern Teheran). He worked as a physician at a hospital in Baghdad and at the courts of several provincial rulers. (5) Al-Fārābī (873–950), "the second Teacher" (Aristotle being the first), was born in Turkestan, but eventually came to Baghdad and studied philosophy and other Greek sciences. How he supported himself is not clear, but he lived an ascetic life and may have needed little. In his closing years he was at the court of Sayf-ad-Dawla of Aleppo (*regnabat* 944–967), occupied in writing books and teaching.[7] (6) Close to the philosophical circle stood the widely-travelled bookseller Ibn-an-Nadīm (d. *c.* 996), whose *Fihrist* or *Catalogue* (of all existing Arabic books known to him, with biographical notes on the authors) is a mine of information about many subjects, including the philosophical movement here described. (7) A minor figure was ʿĪsā (d. 1001), son of the "good vizier" ʿAlī ibn-ʿĪsā. He was a secretary to the caliphs, and one of the few men in the philosophical circles of whom we know definitely that he had made some study of the Islamic

sciences, in particular of Tradition.

(8) From at least about 980 there flourished in Baghdad a most varied philosophical circle, meeting in the house of Abū-Sulaymān as-Sijistānī, "the logician" (d. after 1001). Students from many different backgrounds interested in one or other of the Greek sciences met and discussed topics of literary, scientific or philosophical interest. Though Abū-Sulaymān stood well in the eyes of the Buwayhid prince ʿAḍud-ad-Dawla (*regnabat in Baghdad* 977–983), he appears to have held no official post but to have lived in retirement, apart from the meetings in his house. (9) Some of these discussions have been described by the host's younger friend, Abū-Ḥayyān at-Taw'ḥīdī (d. after 1010). This man was a Persian with Muʿtazilite leanings, and a man of letters rather than a philosopher; he also knew something of Islamic law. By profession he was a scribe and amanuensis, latterly serving as secretary to viziers and other court officials in Baghdad and the provinces.

(10) Ibn-Khammār (d. 1017), a Christian who became a Muslim, was a physician and philosopher who latterly was at the courts of Khwarizm and Ghazna in the east. (11) Another man who was not exactly a philosopher was the Persian Miskawayh (d. 1030), who was secretary and librarian to several viziers. (12) A man with considerable philosophical talent was "the Ṣāḥib", Ibn-ʿAbbād (d. 995), the son of a secretary in Rayy, who rose to be vizier there and made himself semi-independent. (13) Ibn-Hindū (d. after 1018), another Persian, though perhaps of Indian extraction, was a secretary of Persian princes.

(14) The great Ibn-Ṣīnā or Avicenna (980–1037), probably another Persian, was the son of a minor administrator in Transoxiana under the Samānid dynasty. His first interest in philosophy came from a Fāṭimid propagandist, though he also had some traditional Islamic

instruction. An otherwise unknown teacher introduced him to the works of the Greek philosophers and scientists, and he continued to read them by himself until he had fully mastered their contents. The chance purchase of a book by al-Fārābī gave him fresh insight, which completed his philosophical development. He worked as a high minister of state at various courts in the unsettled times of the early eleventh century.[8] (15) Shortly after these men a self-taught physician and philosopher appears in Cairo, Ibn-Riḍwān (d. 1061).[9] (16) Abū-'l-Ḥasan Sa'īd Hibatallāh (d. 1102) was physician in charge of a hospital in Baghdad and also a philosopher. (17) Ibn-Jazla (d. 1100), a pupil of the last-named, was originally a Christian, but was persuaded by his Mu'tazilite instructor in logic, Abū-'Alī ibn-al-Walīd, to become a Muslim. He subsequently obtained an official post at the law-courts.

What stands out clearly from this list is that the bearers of the Greek sciences and the new Islamic philosophy were quite different from the bearers of Islamic religious learning.

Only in one or two cases are men with a competence in philosophy reported to have made any advanced study of Traditions or the Sharī'a; and it may be that even these few had not progressed far. Moreover, those who pursued philosophical studies, unless they were doctors or found a patron at some court, were unable to gain a living from their studies but had to work as secretaries or in humbler ways. For philosophy to flourish as it did there must have been many enthusiasts among them.

The close link between the philosophical movement and the class of secretaries or civil servants suggests the question whether there is any connection between this attraction of philosophy for them in the tenth and eleventh centuries and the interest they showed in

Manichaeanism in the eighth century. Then it seems probable that the class of secretaries, conscious that from Sasanian times they had been the bearers of Perso-Iraqian culture, saw in Manichaeanism a basis from which to criticize the growing class of Islamic scholar-jurists, which was threatening to become a dangerous rival.[10] In the tenth and eleventh centuries this rivalry still existed, and philosophy also might provide a basis for criticism; but the next section will show that there is little that can be called an attack on the scholar-jurists, only attempts at self-justification with a view to self-preservation. If there is anything in the suggestion above that the rulers interested in philosophy were anxious to reduce their dependence on the scholar-jurists, their support of the secretary-philosophers would coalesce with the latter's effort to remain independent. What has been said in this paragraph is all somewhat conjectural, but it does not affect the fact of the link between the secretaries and the philosophical movement.

The essence of the situation was that there were two separate educational systems in the Islamic empire, the old Greek one and the new Islamic one. It was not unlike the situation in most Islamic countries during the past century, when there was the traditional Islamic educational system with its crown in universities like al-Az'har in Cairo and a modern system culminating in Western-style universities. The parallel must not be pressed too far, however. There was much less organization in medieval times, and in particular the study of Greek science and philosophy was hardly organized at all except at the teaching hospitals, and it is doubtful whether we are justified in speaking of a philosophical school or college at Baghdad except in the sense that there was a group of like-minded people. There was certainly such a group, however, and there was certainly continuity in their thought. Before trying to say any more about them we must consider some of the things they themselves said.

2 THE SOCIAL RELEVANCE OF PHILOSOPHICAL IDEAS

One of the basic conceptions of this study is that, whether men are aware of it or not, their ideas reflect social facts and social aspirations. Plato had an understanding of our problem, and in the *Republic* gives prominence to the parallelism between an individual's powers and the class-structure of society. The ideal state for him was one where the intellectuals were the ruling class, and in accordance with this view he engaged in politics to the extent of trying to make the ruler of a small state a philosopher-prince. Yet he was also aware of the difficulty of realizing this ideal in practice. There is another strand in his thought which distinguishes between the unchanging world of the forms and the ordinary world of becoming and dissolution, *genesis* and *phthora*. According to this strand of his thought the proper work of the intellect or reason—and so, we infer, of the intellectual—is not in controlling the mutable things of space and time, but in dealing with the immutable forms; in other words, the intellectuals contract out of politics, and leave public affairs to those who have the knack. The allegory of the cave in the *Republic* attempts to explain why the philosophers, who know the realities of which the shadows are seen in the cave, are often worse at dealing with the shadows than those who have not philosophized. These strands were still present in the Greek philosophical tradition when, more than a millennium after Plato, it thrust itself upon the Muslims;[11] and the position of philosophers in Hellenistic and Byzantine society was a factor, even if a minor one, in determining the place of philosophers in Islamic society.

(a) *Ar-Rāzī*

In surveying the social implications of Islamic philosophical thought it is convenient to begin with ar-Rāzī (d. 923 or 932), though he was younger than al-Kindī. He stands somewhat apart from the other great philosophers of Islam, being less under the influence of Proclus than they.

Ar-Rāzī accepts the Platonic conception of the soul as tripartite,[12] which implies the superiority of reason; and he has much to say about the control of the passions by reason. Reason is also the source of all civilized life:

"God gave us reason, chiefly that we might attain the utmost benefits we are capable of, both temporal and eternal. It is the greatest of God's gifts; nothing is more profitable for us. By Reason we are superior to the brute beasts; we subjugate them, and employ them in ways useful both to us and them. By Reason we apprehend all that elevates us, and beautifies and enriches our life; by it we attain our heart's desire. By Reason we learn how to build and sail ships, and thereby reach lands beyond the seas. By it we acquire the medical art, to the great advantage of our bodies, and the other useful arts. By it we apprehend what is obscure, far-off and concealed. By it we know the shape of earth and sky, and the magnitude, distance and motions of sun, moon and stars. By it we come to knowledge of the Creator, the summit of our comprehension and chief source of our welfare. In short, without Reason our condition would be that of beasts, children and madmen."[13]

Despite this realization of the contribution of Reason to the fabric of the life of the community, ar-Rāzī shows no desire that reason should guide and control political affairs. He advises people not to try to raise their status by engaging in politics. He defends himself against the charge of having consorted with princes, by pointing out that he has held no appointment in the army or civil service, but has merely treated the prince's body when he was ill, and given him counsel in health. He has not aimed at increasing his wealth, but has been content with a modest sufficiency; and we know that he must have worked incessantly at his medical and other scientific studies and in writing his numerous books. His ideal is what he calls "the philosophic life", a life of intellectual activity. The rational part of the soul falls short of its true nature unless it "sees the wonder and grandeur of the world, meditates on it and marvels at it, and has an insatiable desire for knowledge of all that is in it, especially the science of the body in which it finds itself and its shape and condition after death".[14]

The most positive things he has to say about political life are in a little essay entitled *The Signs of Worldly Advancement and Political Power*. The theme of this is that certain people are marked out to be rulers of men. Nature has endowed them with qualities of character such as nobility and perhaps a certain personal magnetism which make others follow them and accept them as leaders. That such people should actually rule he regards as right and proper. In this he seems to be inclining to fatalism, for there is something ineluctable about these differences fixed by "nature". This is not altogether consistent with his general view of reason. At other times, however, he maintains that all men are equally endowed with reason, and on this ground argues against the conception of God sending prophets, since these give knowledge to some people and not to others. This is implicitly an attack on the existing Islamic basis of society.

In general, ar-Rāzī's version of Platonism becomes a justification for the kind of life he was leading, a life of intellectual, mainly scientific, pursuits apart from the main stream of society. His philosophy enabled him to think and feel that he was doing something significant. He was allowing the highest or rational part of him to live its proper life. To put it in another way, the aim of human life is to become as like God as possible; God is all-knowing, all-just and all-merciful; and so man must endeavour to grow in knowledge, justice and mercy.[15] Knowledge, we observe, comes first. From our vantage-point of over ten centuries later we can see that ar-Rāzī was indeed playing a most important part in the life of Islamic society, but his theory did not account for all he was in fact achieving, nor was he himself aware of its full importance.

(b) *Al-Kindī*

The most distinctive and most important line in Islamic philosophy—to be roughly described as Neoplatonism on a basis of Aristotelian logic—begins with al-Kindī (d. 866) and leads on to al-Fārābī and Avicenna. Al-Kindī's thought has many similarities with that of ar-Rāzī. He considers it one of the functions of reason, or rather of the soul, to control the passions; and he emphasizes the distinction between the transient things which are the objects of the passions or sensuous desires, and the lasting good which is the object of rational desire. On the other hand, his conception of the soul (*nafs*) is more developed and more Aristotelian than that of ar-Rāzī. Among the points he makes in his *Essay on the Soul* are that it restrains anger and desire, that it persists after death, that when it is purified it has true knowledge of things, and that its true habitation is in the higher supernal world (*ʿālam ar-rubūbiyya*).[16] This is still not unlike ar-Rāzī; but his *Essay on the*

Reason is explicitly Aristotelian and leads on to al-Fārābī's fuller work with the same title.[17] The conception of emanation (*fayḍ*) frequently occurs; and God is spoken of as the only true agent, the only one who acts upon others but is not himself acted upon.[18]

The relation of these ideas to their social context is not obvious so long as we look only at al-Kindī, but it becomes apparent when we notice how al-Fārābī treated them. What is remarkable in al-Kindī is the absence of any sense of conflict or tension between philosophy and the Islamic sciences. Unlike ar-Rāzī, who criticized the conception of prophethood, al-Kindī always speaks as a good Muslim. He asserts that the knowledge brought by truthful prophets is identical with the results of "first philosophy" or metaphysics; and he interprets the Qur'ān in terms of the Greek scientific world-view.[19] On the practical side, he holds that the soul which has been illuminated is entrusted by God with the conduct of political affairs.[20] In all this al-Kindī probably reflects the political situation from about 820 to 850, when many of the highest posts were held by men of Muʿtazilite views and when the caliphs also had leanings in this direction. The Muʿtazilites were Islamic theologians with a moderate knowledge of Greek philosophy. Thus the caliphate was in fact being administered by a group of intellectuals of whom al-Kindī could approve. He himself was much more fully acquainted with Greek learning and less interested in theology and less involved in politics. This seems to explain why his works show no awareness of the underlying tensions between philosophers and scholar-jurists.

(c) *Al-Fārābī*

The political implications in the Islamic world of the Neoplatonic conception of emanation become clear in the thought of al-Fārābī (d. 950), who has left several works on politics. According to this concept the universe is hierarchical in the sense that at its summit is the most perfect being, the being that most truly is, and that from this being proceed less perfect beings and from these a lower grade of being until the lowest of all is reached. In the same way al-Fārābī regards the city or civilized community as hierarchical. At the summit is the head or leader (*ra'īs*). Then come the leaders of second rank, then those of the third, until the lowest rank is reached consisting of those who follow others but do not themselves lead any others. The supreme leader is he who leads or commands or controls others, but is not himself led or commanded or controlled by others.

There are various points to be noticed about this conception of the state. Firstly, the qualities which mark out the leader are not purely rational or intellectual. Al-Fārābī has a long list of the qualities required by the supreme leader, and they include moral excellences and gifts of personality. One is reminded of ar-Rāzī's view that some men are naturally marked out to be leaders. By thus widening the conception of reason al-Fārābī brings his theory close to the political facts of his time, though, as we shall see, he regards his conception of the state as an ideal seldom to be realized. Secondly, al-Fārābī's account of the state is not far removed from the old ideas of autocratic sovereignty associated with the east. The supreme leader is the source of the whole life of the state. This fits exactly some of the early conceptions of the divine kingship in the Middle East.[21] It also fits the contemporary practice.

"The grades of the people of the city in leadership or service are higher or lower according to their natural disposition and upbringing. The first leader grades the group; and every man in every group is in the grade of which he is worthy, either of service or of leadership.

. . . The leader, after assigning these grades, when he wants something different, can make fresh ordinances. . . ."[22]

This activity of the first leader is exactly that of the caliph. In the ʿAbbāsid state (as contrasted with the Umayyad) inherited nobility counted for little, whether it was that of the pre-Islamic Arab aristocracy or that of the Islamic families ennobled by the stipend system and similar measures. The ʿAbbāsid court consisted of men who had been given positions by the caliph for their own merits and usefulness (even if some were also sons of courtiers), and they could be removed from their positions just as easily as they could be placed in them. They were the caliph's creations.

In all this al-Fārābī's views are close to those of the Shīʿites, who also emphasize the leader. Yet there is a difference, for the leader sought by the Shīʿites was one with charismata which were independent of any personal effort of his and which placed him in a category above ordinary men. It is possible to take al-Fārābī's views in a Shīʿite sense, but it is not necessary to do so, and therefore it would be wrong to infer from his conception of the state that he had Shīʿite leanings.[23]

The idea, then, of the emanation of all being from the supreme Being, apart from its attractiveness as a harmonious world-view embracing all the science of the day, appealed to the deep-seated tradition of autocratic rule and the ordinary (educated) man's sense of being dependent on some one above him. Al-Fārābī, however, modifies strict logic to make his thought accord better with the historical situation of his day. The supreme leader is described as a prophet-philosopher.[24]

"When that occurs (the inherence of the active reason in a man) in both parts of his rational faculty, speculative and practical, and then in his imaginative faculty, that man is the one to whom revelation is given, and it is God who reveals to him by means of the active reason; what flows (or emanates) from God to the active reason, the active reason pours into his passive reason by means of the acquired reason, and then into his imaginative faculty. By what is poured into his passive reason he becomes wise, a philosopher, altogether prudent; by what is poured into his imaginative faculty, he becomes a prophet, warning about what will be, and announcing the particulars which now are. . . . Such a man is in the most perfect grade of humanity, and in the highest degree of happiness. . . ."

One difficulty caused by thus making the supreme leader a prophet is that, according to the standard Sunnite view, there has been no prophet in the Islamic state since Muḥammad. Al-Fārābī has therefore to justify the following of Muḥammad's example although he has been long dead. After the above description of the "first leader" or prophet-philosopher and a list of thirteen qualities he ought to have, there comes an account of the "second leader" who "follows" the first.[25] This is not a second-in-command but a successor. The Arabic word translated "follow", *yakhlufu*, has the connotation of following as a deputy, vicegerent or replacement, that is, as a caliph, *khalīfa*. This successor has to have six qualities. He must be wise (that is, a philosopher); he must know and remember and follow the revealed-laws, customs and manner of life (*sharā'i'*, *sunan*, *siyar*) established for the state by the "first ones"; he must be good at deducing new applications for their principles; he must be good at devising experimental ways of dealing with entirely new situations; he must be good at persuading people to accept his policies; he must be able to endure the hardships of war. Al-Fārābī then continues:

"If there is no one man in whom all these conditions are fulfilled but if there are two, one with wisdom (philosophy), and the other with the remaining qualities, then these two should be leaders in this city. If the qualities are distributed among a group, so that one has wisdom, another the second quality, another the third, and so on, and if the men are mutually suitable, they should be the superior leaders. When it happens at some time that wisdom (philosophy) is not a part of the leadership . . . the virtuous city remains without a king. . . ."

This is an attempt to bring the description of the ideal state within measurable distance of the actual state. One important point to notice is that in all these discussions there is complete acceptance of the Islamic basis of the state. The supreme leader has to be portrayed with the features of the prophet Muḥammad. Even for a philosopher like al-Fārābī there is no conceivable alternative to the existing Islamic state. What he does try to maintain is that the philosophers should have a say in the running of the state comparable to that of the scholar-jurists. The second and third qualities of the "second leader" seem to be meant to be those of the Traditionists and scholar-jurists; and the suggestion is that, when the qualities are divided out, the bearers of each quality are approximately equal. In so far as philosophers had a position at court (or in the civil service) and were able to influence the ruler (central or provincial) by their advice, there was some truth in this claim for the philosophers; but on the whole their influence must have been decreasing and that of the scholar-jurists increasing.

While this conclusion is to be drawn from the passage quoted above, another passage shows that al-Fārābī regarded the work of the philosopher as more fundamental than that of the scholar-jurist.[26] Knowledge is required by the citizens of the virtuous state, but this may be of two kinds, either "conceiving", "rational conception", or "imaging", "imaginative understanding". Most men are unable to have a rational conception of what as citizens they need to know, such as the ultimate principles of existing things and their hierarchical order, the nature of happiness and of supreme leadership in the state, and the particular acts conducive to happiness. For such men the higher powers produce symbols and images by means of the prophets, and these symbols and images may vary from people to people and religion to religion, some being better than others, but the things themselves are the same for all. Here al-Fārābī is trying to exalt the philosopher, who handles absolute truth, above the scholar-jurist, whose material has only relative truth. Is this perhaps because he realizes that the scholar-jurists have more actual influence than the philosophers?

Altogether al-Fārābī is a fascinating author on the subject of politics. He fully accepts the Islamic state, but interprets it in Neoplatonic terms. He tries hard to make a place in his scheme for the scholar-jurists, and in some passages succeeds; but at other times he is unable to conceal his essential belief that the real successors of the Platonic intellectuals are the philosophers in the Greek tradition.

(d) *Avicenna*

The physician and philosopher Avicenna or Ibn-Sīnā (d. 1037) worked out a philosophical system on similar lines to al-Fārābī, to whose books he acknowledged his indebtedness. He is generally reckoned the more profound philosopher of the two. Among the similarities which specially concern the present study are the full acceptance of the Islamic state system and the framing of a theory of prophecy in terms of Neoplatonic epistemology. Since his epistemology differs slightly from that of his predecessor, it is only natural that there are some small differences in the theory of prophecy. He also takes the view that for ordinary people, who are mostly incapable of philosophic thinking, religion must be expressed in symbolic form.

He differs from al-Fārābī, however, in various ways. In general he has far less to say about politics. He apparently never discusses the question of "second leaders", but instead regards it as part of the office of the prophet to make provision for the maintenance of his religious and social system after his death. On the whole, the position of the prophet is enhanced. Prophets are a rare phenomenon. Prophetic apprehension of truth, though it may come about instantaneously, is not authority-based (*taqlīdī*) but rational (*ʿaqlī*).[27] The work of the prophet, too, is more fundamental than that of the philosopher, since it is absolutely essential for the welfare of the state. Only the formulations of the prophet give ordinary people the knowledge requisite if the state is to prosper. In so far as the philosophers' formulations are comprehensible only to the few, the philosophers would seem to be less useful.[28]

The differences between Avicenna and al-Fārābī may be linked up with certain differences in their historical situations. Al-Fārābī had died in 950, whereas Avicenna's life stretched from 980 to 1037. In 969 the Fāṭimids from Tunisia had conquered Egypt, and soon afterwards founded Cairo to be their capital. They claimed to be the rightful caliphs or leaders of the whole community of Muslims, and without delay began to send out emissaries eastwards to work for the overthrow of the ʿAbbāsid caliphate by the dissemination of Fāṭimid-Ismāʿīlite propaganda. This propaganda doubtless also threatened the autonomous states subordinate to the caliphate. Even the Shīʿites in the ʿAbbāsid domains (including the Buwayhid sultans in Baghdad) would be threatened, since practically none of them accepted the

Ismāʿīlite form of Shīʿism. Now much of al-Fārābī's political philosophy, even if he himself was not a Shīʿite, was capable of being used to justify Shīʿite and indeed Fāṭimid policies. He tended to place the emphasis on the actual leader or ruler of the state in the present. Avicenna, on the other hand, says nothing about the flow of divine wisdom into and through the actual ruler. His emphasis is on the founding of the Islamic religion and community by Muḥammad nearly four centuries earlier. This is much more of a Sunnite position, and not unlike that adopted by al-Ghazālī towards the Ismāʿīlites.

Another fact to be remembered about Avicenna is that he had a prominent place at various minor courts in the east of the caliphate, such as Bukhara, Gurganj, Hamadhan and Ispahan, sometimes even being vizier or chief minister. Thus he had as much political power as he wanted, and sometimes refused appointments. His relation to the governments under which he served is not unlike that of the Muʿtazilites of Baghdad in the period round about the caliphate of al-Ma'mūn (813–833). It is therefore significant that both he and the Muʿtazilites should think that their interpretation of Islam in terms of Greek thought was a genuine account of traditional Islam. (Avicenna's account, of course, was much more philosophical than that of the Muʿtazilites.) In so far as they, philosophically minded men, had more political influence than the scholar-jurists, they were able to present their philosophical interpretation of Islam as the standard interpretation. There was no need to exaggerate the importance of philosophy because there was no need to seek greater political influence for philosophically-minded men.

Avicenna was also attracted to mysticism. What is the explanation of this? Can it in any way be regarded as a reaction to political impotence? He was not altogether impotent, but he lived in a very disturbed period and may well have felt that any good work a man might do was liable to be swept away by a sudden change in the current of fortune. In his *Autobiography* he tells how he had just managed to reach a point from which he could have approached Qābūs, the ruler of Gurgan and Ṭabaristan, when the latter was taken prisoner and died; he would doubtless have proved an enlightened patron. Avicenna must also have felt that little of lasting importance could be achieved by political action. He has therefore no romantic hopes of a reform of the existing state system by statesmen, however philosophical. Instead he turns to the cultivation of the inner life. He sometimes speaks about three stages, those of the ascetic, the worshipper and the "gnostic" (*zāhid*, *'ābid*, *'ārif*), and describes the last stage in detail.[29] This was clearly an important part of his own experience. It may have been in part an expression of his despair of historical achievement, but much more it seems to spring from a realization that the significance of life is to be found beyond history.

(e) *Abū-Sulaymān al-Manṭiqī as-Sijistānī*

A contrary reaction to that of Avicenna is possibly shown by Abū-Sulaymān of Sijistān (d. 1001), known as "the logician". The explanation may lie in the fact that he and most of the coterie which met in his house were comparatively uninfluential politically. An account has been preserved of a meeting after the death of the Buwayhid sultan 'Aḍud-ad-Dawla in 983, when they emulated the ten philosophers who made epigrams on the death of Alexander.[30] Abū-Sulaymān opened with a severe criticism of the deceased ruler: "This person weighed the world in an improper scale, and assigned it an undue price. It is enough that seeking profit in the world he lost his soul." After the others had spoken he quoted from the official Friday sermon when the death was announced:

"What hast thou accomplished with thy goods and slaves and retainers and army, with thy stored wealth and keen wit? Why didst thou not make a friend of Him who set thee on the throne, and bestow all on Him? . . . He knew thy weakness who designed thy fall, and they little knew thee who thought thee mighty! Nay, He made thee king who ruined thee with sovereignty, and He dethroned thee who designed thy doom! Truly thou art a warning to all that will be warned, and a sign to all that have eyes to see!"

Now ʿAḍud-ad-Dawla is generally reckoned a strong and successful ruler by modern historians, though he was not able to prevent his family from quarrelling after his death about the succession; and the bitterness of the criticism is surprising. It is reminiscent of some earlier criticisms of the caliphs by scholar-jurists. What seems most likely is that Abū-Sulaymān and his friends, feeling that their merits were not given sufficient public recognition, were withdrawing into themselves, and at the same time asserting the superiority of their philosophical way of life.

3 AL-GHAZĀLĪ'S PERIOD OF SCEPTICISM

After this examination of the progress of philosophy in the Islamic world, it is possible to appreciate better al-Ghazālī's description of the period of scepticism through which he passed. It is convenient to begin with an abbreviated version of what he says in his autobiographical work *Deliverance from Error*.[31] He begins by saying to a "brother in religion" that he will try to tell him what he has found in his quest for truth, and explains how from his earliest youth he tried to have a genuine understanding of the various sects and religious movements with which he came in contact, and how he was puzzled by the fact that men appear to become Jews or Christians or Muslims because of environmental influences. He wondered how the beliefs acquired from parents and teachers could be tested for their truth, and whether there was a natural religion prior to these environmental influences.

"I said to myself, I am seeking knowledge of what things really are, so I must know what knowledge is. I saw that certain knowledge must exclude all doubt and the possibility of error, indeed even the supposition of this. The person who performs miracles should not be able to shake one's conviction of the truth of such knowledge. For example, if someone says, 'Three is greater than ten, and the proof is that I shall turn this rod into a serpent', and if he actually does it in my presence, I still do not doubt my knowledge, but only wonder how he achieved the transformation. From such considerations I realized that only where I have an unshakable conviction of this kind is my knowledge certain knowledge.

"When I examined my knowledge, I found that none of it was certain except matters of sense-perception and necessary truths. It further occurred to me, however, that my present trust in sense-perception and necessary truths was perhaps no better founded than my previous trust in propositions accepted from parents and teachers. So I earnestly set about making myself doubt sense-perception and necessary truths. With regard to sense-perception I noticed that the sense of sight tells me that the shadow cast by the gnomon of a sundial is motionless; but later observation and reflection shows that it moves, and that it does so not by jerks but by a constant steady motion. This sense also tells me that the sun is the size of a coin, but astronomical proofs show that it is larger than the earth. Thus sense makes certain judgements, and then reason comes and judges that they are false.

"I said to myself, 'Since my trust in sense-perception has proved vain, perhaps all that is to be relied on are rational propositions and first principles, such as that ten is more than three, that negation and affirmation cannot both hold of anything, that a thing cannot be both originated-in-time and eternal, both existent and non-existent, necessary and impossible'. Then sense-perception said, 'Do you not expect that your trust in rational propositions will fare like your trust in sense-perception? You used to trust in me, but Judge Reason came and showed I was false. Perhaps beyond rational apprehension there will be another judge; when he appears he will show that reason is false. The fact that this supra-rational apprehension has not appeared yet, does not show that it is impossible.'

"While my self was hesitating about the reply to this, sense-perception increased its difficulties by a reference to dreams, and said, 'In dreams you imagine things, and you believe that they are real and genuine so long as you are in the dream-state; but when you wake, you know that what you have been imagining has no basis in reality. How are you sure of the real existence of all that you believe in your waking state through sense or reason? It is true in relation to your present state; but another state may come upon you, whose relation to your present waking state is like the relation of that state to the dream state; in short, your present state will be like a dream in relation to that state. If this state comes, you will be certain that all your rational suppositions are baseless imaginings. Perhaps this is the "state" of the ṣūfīs in which they claim that they see things which are not in accordance with rational principles. Perhaps this state is death, and perhaps this life is a dream in relation to the life to come, so that, when a man dies, things will become apparent to him which are contrary to what he now observes.'

"When these thoughts occurred to me, I tried to find a remedy for them, but it was not easy. They could not be disproved, for a proof has to be based on first principles, and here it was the truth of first principles which was in question. The illness proved a difficult one. It lasted almost two months. During this time I was a sceptic in fact, though not in outward expression. Then God healed me from this disease. My self was restored to a sound and balanced condition. The necessary truths of reason became once again accepted and trusted in with complete certainty. That did not come about through proof or argument, but by a light which God cast into my breast; that light is the key to most knowledge. To suppose that the understanding of profound truth rests upon marshalled arguments is to narrow unduly the broad mercy of God. As Muḥammad said, 'God created the creatures in darkness, and later sprinkled on them some of his light'. It is from this light that deep understanding must be sought. That light floods out from the Divine generosity at certain times, and one must be on the watch for it.

"The point of this narrative is to show that one has gone to the utmost in seeking truth, when one stops short of first principles. First principles are not to be sought, since they are already present; and when what is present is sought, it becomes lost and hidden. If a man only looks for what may properly be looked for, he cannot be accused of falling short in the quest for truth."

The first thing to be said in considering this account of an attack of scepticism is that *Deliverance from Error*, though autobiographical, is not strictly an autobiography. In particular, it cannot be accepted as an accurate chronological record of events. Immediately after the long passage which has just been paraphrased, al-Ghazālī says he now regarded the seekers after truth as divided into four groups, theologians, Bāṭinites, philosophers and ṣūfīs; and he proceeded to study the views of each group thoroughly in order to arrive at truth for himself. This must be a literary fiction—a convenient framework for a schematic presentation of his conclusions. It seems unlikely that the period of scepticism occurred at an early stage in his theological studies. It seems certain that the fit of scepticism as he describes it must have been preceded by some study of philosophy. It is also clear that he had contacts with mysticism at a comparatively early period.[32] Thus the plan of *Deliverance from Error* must be regarded as schematic and not chronological. There is no reason, however, to doubt that he had an actual experience such as he describes. What we cannot say is that it came early in his career; it may well have been about the time of his move to Baghdad in 1091, since we know that it was shortly after this that he was engaged in the intensive study of philosophy. It is also probable that his experience led him to a complete reappraisal of all the departments of his knowledge.

That al-Ghazālī's scepticism had a philosophical background is shown by the fact that he links it up with a consideration of the nature of knowledge and certainty. Some of his arguments bear a close resemblance to those used, albeit for another purpose, by Miskawayh (d. 1030). The latter speaks of the "judgement" of sense by reason, and among the examples he includes that of the sun, which is known by rational proofs to be a hundred and sixty odd times greater than the earth.[33] It is not necessary to maintain that al-Ghazālī had read this particular passage, though he may well have done so. This passage shows that one of the points made by al-Ghazālī was being discussed by philosophers in the Islamic world shortly before his time. Apart from this specific evidence, the critique of knowledge is an aspect of philosophy. The Platonic tradition, too, which was so strong in the Arabic-writing philosophers, has suggestions of a sphere above reason, or at least above ordinary mundane reason.[34]

The reason which al-Ghazālī is criticizing is primarily reason in its theological use. This is indicated by the example he uses of a man trying to prove that three is more than ten by performing a miracle. This was exactly the argument used by Islamic theology. A prophet, according to the theologians, comes to his people with a message from God, and says to them, "This is a message from God, and the proof that it is from God is that such and such a miracle will happen". The underlying idea is that a miracle, since it involves a breach in the order of nature, can only be produced by supernatural power. God produces breaches of the normal order to substantiate the claims of genuine prophets sent by himself; but if anyone falsely claims to have a message from God, it will not be substantiated by a miracle.[35] In other words, al-Ghazālī's scepticism must have been due in part to a realization that the rational arguments at the foundation of Islamic theology were not fully rational, but rested on many assumptions which could not be rationally justified. Until this time al-Ghazālī must have thought of reason as being exemplified above all in theology, not philosophy. In his book *The Aims of the Philosophers*, in which he gave an objective statement of their doctrines without criticism, he has a revealing sentence to the effect that "there is nothing in the conclusions of solid geometry and arithmetic which is contrary to reason".[36] For a philosophically-minded person these would have been the most prominent examples of the use of reason! What he means is that mathematical propositions are not contrary to rational theology.

Did this scepticism about reason in its theological use also extend to it in its philosophical use? Whether it did so or not during the two months' crisis we cannot be sure, but it is not impossible that his doubts were about reason in all its uses. The remarks at the end of the passage quoted about looking only for what may properly be looked for, suggest familiarity with the syllogism and with the fact that the first premisses of a series of syllogisms cannot be syllogistically proved. In due course, as we know from the passage about philosophy in *Deliverance from Error*, he came to see that the metaphysical and theological aspects of philosophy are far from satisfying the canons of strict demonstration set up by the logicians. Thus, whatever the relative dating, his scepticism was eventually turned against philosophy as well as theology.

A similar conclusion is reached by another line of approach. The question may be asked whether there was ever a time when al-Ghazālī was tempted to abandon theology for philosophy. The process of answering it will lead into a consideration of some of the more profound implications of his scepticism.

The attraction of philosophy at that period might be compared to that of science at the present time. One outstanding difference was that, whereas our science has had to cut itself adrift from much of the philosophical tradition of Europe, science in the Islamic world was intimately associated with the most coherent philosophical system of the day. Medicine and astronomy-astrology were important in practical life, and logical theory could not but appeal, even if only aesthetically, to argumentative theologians. Thus there could be no question of abandoning these sciences altogether. The dual system of education, however, tended to make men either predominantly "Greek" in their outlook and adherents of philosophy or else predominantly Islamic and largely ignorant of Greek learning. There was little interaction between the two intellectual traditions. Up to this time there had been only a partial infusion of Greek thought into Islamic theology—that effected by the great Muʿtazilites about the time of al-Maʾmūn (*regnabat* 813–833). What was then assimilated had been retained by the theologians, but they had done little to come to terms with the much more fully developed philosophy of al-Fārābī and Avicenna. At most some of them, probably including al-Juwaynī, had read a few books.

The philosophers, on the other hand, as we have seen, had completely accepted the Islamic state and given it a place in their system. If we may trust al-Ghazālī's expositions of their arguments, they frequently supported their statements by quotations from the Qurʾān;[37] and they were prepared to allow the scholar-jurists a function as mediators between the prophet and the ordinary people.[38] Even with all this, however, there was a deep inner contradiction in their view. Avicenna went so far as to say that the "transcendent faculty" (*quwwa qudsiyya*) of the prophet is "the highest of the grades of the human faculties";[39] and this seems to imply that the prophet is the summit of human achievement. Yet the philosophical dogma of the supremacy of reason is in conflict with this. If reason is supreme, how can the prophet rather than the philosopher be the ideal man? If the prophet is supreme, how can philosophical reason presume to sit in judgement on his words? As al-Ghazālī remarks, the philosopher has succumbed to false pride in his achievements in "supposing that divine things can be absolutely subject to his thought and imagination".[40] The contradiction is also seen in the fact that the whole texture of the life of the state is governed by Islamic ideas. There are indeed "Greek" ethical works in Arabic (such as that of Miskawayh), but the "Greek" ethico-political system was far from providing a viable alternative to the actual Islamic system.

Thus philosophical reason, despite its claims, was not really an alternative to the corpus of Islamic thought. Al-Ghazālī, educated in the latter, cannot but have felt this.

These deeper reasons probably influenced al-Ghazālī most, but there were also more superficial ones. The philosophers were a small coterie—almost of cranks and eccentrics, had it not been that some were excellent physicians. They were divided among themselves. Even if some had high offices in political administration, they had little influence as a group. Many good Muslims looked on them with profound suspicion, and even attacked reputable theologians for meddling with their books.[41] Only with very strong motives could a theologian have defied this heritage of suspicion and joined the ranks of the philosophers. All in all, it seems most unlikely that al-Ghazālī was ever seriously tempted to leave theology for philosophy.

From all this it follows, if the argument is sound, that at the root of al-Ghazālī's scepticism was a largely unconscious disquiet with something in the contemporary condition of rational theology. At most philosophy had contributed to increase the disquiet, and to focus it on the imperfect rationality of theology. But there must have been something in theology itself, or in the theologians, that first made it possible for al-Ghazālī to entertain such doubts. He had been trained to expect a career as a scholar-jurist (that of a theologian was merely a branch of this general career—he also wrote one or two books on law). His scepticism must therefore mean that he had grave doubts about the career. Was it due to some weakness in himself? Not unless too great honesty for coping with a wicked world is a weakness. What happened later, however, and an analysis of his criticisms of the scholar-jurists of his day, makes it clear that it was nothing personal that made him a sceptic.

The full examination of this matter belongs to a later

chapter. Here some preliminary points may be noted. Let it be assumed that the source of al-Ghazālī's disquiet was the failure in some respects (not yet specified) of the scholar-jurists. As a zealous young man connected with the movement of religious revival (in an external sense) directed by Niẓām-al-Mulk, he would wonder how this state of things could be improved, and he would find the resources of the theological tradition very meagre. His scepticism may be seen as a realization of the inability of reason (or human planning) to set things right. It is in accordance with this interpretation that the solution of the crisis, as he describes it, is found by no human effort but comes from "a light which God cast into my breast". Man does what he can, but realizes his inability to proceed, and then, as he pauses baffled, something beyond himself sets his feet on a new path forward. Just what the light was, al-Ghazālī does not say. In another passage of *Deliverance from Error*, however, he says that when he approached the study of ṣūfism he already had a settled belief in God, prophethood and the Last Day.[42] This is probably not the precise form in which the illumination ending his scepticism came to him, but it may be the working out of that illumination.

There are various other small indications that al-Ghazālī's disquiet was essentially a feeling that his civilization was facing a crisis and the solution was neither to hand nor obvious. When he had recovered from his scepticism, he began a quest for truth by examining the teachings of the four main groups of "seekers for truth"; he thereby implied that both he and they lacked some important aspect of truth. The title of his book, *Deliverance from Error*, has presumably a social as well as an individual reference, and carries the implication that the community has somehow gone astray. And it would not be out of place to note here that the title of his greatest book, *The Revival of the Religious Sciences*, presumes some decadence or decay in these sciences. It is a major aim of this study to try to discover in what this decadence consisted.

Perhaps enough has been said to show how al-Ghazālī was involved in the tensions of his time. The one under consideration in this chapter is that between the two rival educational systems, each trying to provide the ideational basis for the whole community. Each had many good points and also some practical weaknesses. Ultimately what was good in them was complementary, but each tended to claim to be self-sufficient and to belittle or reject the contribution of its rival. Al-Ghazālī did not attempt to escape from this tension. On the contrary he entered more fully into it, until he felt it deeply within himself. The period of scepticism is the internal aspect of the process of resolving the external tension by entering into it. By his voluntary act of accepting this and other tensions into himself al-Ghazālī was able to achieve a resolution of the tensions which affected the whole subsequent history of Islam.

4 "THE INCONSISTENCY OF THE PHILOSOPHERS"

At the end of the previous chapter al-Ghazālī's life-story was taken up to the point of his arrival in Baghdad in July 1091. He then became immersed in his teaching duties, and seems to have been a popular lecturer, for at one time (he tells us in *Deliverance from Error*) he had an audience of three hundred students. We hear of him taking part in the usual official functions.[43] Yet he also found time to obtain a real grasp of the Islamic version of Neoplatonic philosophy and the associated sciences. He did this, too, merely by private reading without any personal contact with philosophers. He was satisfied with his understanding of the subject "in less than two years", but in addition he spent "nearly a year" in reflection on it, doubtless deciding what points in it could be accepted by a theologian and what points had to be rejected.[44] It cannot have been till towards the end of the period of reflection that he began to write the two books to be considered here. The first, *The Aims of the Philosophers*, was a factual and objective account of the doctrines of the Islamic Neoplatonists, following Avicenna for the most part; the second contained his criticisms of the philosophers and was entitled *The Inconsistency of the Philosophers*.[45] One manuscript has a note according to which the book was finished in January 1095; and there is no good reason for rejecting this.[46] If we allow six months for the writing of the two books—which may be too much—he must have finished his time of reflecting on philosophy by July 1094. But, as he spent nearly three years between studying and reflecting, the study must have begun soon after he reached Baghdad in July 1091. That is to say, most of the four years he spent at Baghdad as a professor was spent in either studying or writing about philosophy. This does not, of course, exclude his having had some previous acquaintance with philosophy, especially logic. What he aimed at acquiring in his studies in Baghdad was a knowledge, especially of logic, physics and metaphysics, comparable to that of the exponents of these sciences.

When *The Inconsistency of the Philosophers* is read in the light of what was said in the previous section, the purpose is clear. As he himself puts it, "the aim is to show your inability to make good your claims to knowledge of the truth of things by apodeictic proofs, and to make you doubtful of your claims".[47] In other words, he is pursuing the critique of reason which underlay his bout of scepticism, and is trying to show that reason is not self-sufficient in the field of metaphysics and is unable out of itself to produce a complete world-view. Of the twenty theses for which al-Ghazālī argues in the book, some concern positive philosophical doctrines which he rejects, but seven consist in proving that doctrines held by the philosophers (and sometimes also held by al-Ghazālī) cannot be demonstrated by reason. Reason by itself, he argues, cannot prove that the world has a creator, that two gods are impossible, that God is not a body, that He knows both others and Himself, and that the soul is a self-subsistent entity.[48]

In all this al-Ghazālī was not simply a sceptic, as has sometimes been alleged, though he frankly admits that he is not arguing for any positive views, but has the negative aim of showing that the philosophers are not free from inconsistency and self-contradiction.[49] This limitation of aim is very understandable in his situation. He had come to the conviction that reason is not self-sufficient in either theology or philosophy, but is in a sense subordinate to a "light from God" shed in the heart which is somehow connected with the light given to men by prophetic revelations. He had only begun, however, the arduous process of giving this conviction a satisfactory intellectual expression. The negative aim of *The Inconsistency of the Philosophers* was a necessary preparation for the erection of a building—a clearing of the site—but the ultimate building was not yet planned in detail.[50]

The thirteen theses where al-Ghazālī rejects doctrines of the philosophers lead us into a different realm. On three points—the assertion that the world is everlasting, the denial that God knows particulars, and the denial of bodily resurrection—he adjudges them to be infidels, outside the community of Islam, though on the other points he regards them as merely heretical, that is, as holding views which are mistaken but not so badly mistaken as to exclude from the community.[51] The thirteen points fall roughly into three groups.

The first and largest group is that associated with the philosophers' assertion that the world is everlasting, in the sense of having no beginning. Al-Ghazālī also rejects the further assertions that the world has no end, that the several heavens are living creatures and move by will, that they have a definite goal towards which they move, that their souls know particulars, and that miracles, or breaches of the course of nature, are impossible. He also accuses them of confusion in describing the proceeding or emanating of the world from God as his creating it.[52] The last point shows what had been happening. The philosophers had been adapting Neoplatonic cosmology to Qur'ānic conceptions by equating emanation with creation. This enabled them to say that, though the world had no beginning in time, God was its ground from whom it derived its existence, and in that sense its creator. All Qur'ānic references to creation were therefore to be interpreted in accordance with this account.

The fundamental cleavage between Sunnite Islam and the philosophers was probably that the Sunnites wanted to regard ultimate reality as analogous to a human will, whereas the philosophers conceived of it rather as an impersonal force. One of al-Ghazālī's complaints is that the philosophers make the world come forth from God by some kind of necessity.[53] The same belief in impersonal necessity leads them to deny the possibility of miracles. They make allowance for something analogous to will and other human qualities by ascribing them to the different heavens; but al-Ghazālī has little difficulty in showing that this is merely hypothetical. He is, of course, no crude anthropomorphist. The question at issue between him and the philosophers is whether the ground of all being is more adequately described by human analogies or by analogies from natural forces.

The same opposition appears in the second group. This consists in the philosophers' assertion that God knows only universals and not particulars, and in other assertions involving the conception of God as bare simplicity, namely, that he has no attributes distinct from his essence, that the distinction between genus and differentia does not apply to him, and that he is bare existence without any quiddity or definite character.[54] Now the conception of God as absolute simplicity, with no special relation to particulars, fits in well with the analogy of a natural force. The force of gravity bears upon a body only in respect of the universal features of weight or mass, not in respect of any particular features apart from these, still less in respect of what makes a man a unique human person. The question of God's attributes had been earlier discussed between the main body of the Sunnites and the sect of the Muʿtazilites. The latter, theologians influenced by philosophy, were of a rationalistic turn of mind and denied that such attributes as knowing, hearing, seeing, speaking, willing, had any distinct existence within God's essence. They seem to have been exalting rational tidiness over the richness of religious experience; and in the long run it was the religious experience of ordinary men that triumphed.

The third group consists of the belief that there is no resurrection of bodies, but only a purely spiritual resurrection of souls (with the corollary that there are no bodily pains and pleasures in the future life), and the accompanying belief that souls are naturally immortal. Here we are dealing not with two rival accounts of ultimate reality but with two rival views of human nature. The philosophers held the dualistic or "Greek" view, according to which man consists of soul and body, but the essential man is the soul, and the body only the soul's temporary garment or, as some extremists put it, its tomb. The contrasting monistic or "Semitic" view is that, even if a distinction is allowed between body and soul, the body is just as much the man as the soul.

In all these disputed matters there are seen to be two main points of difference between al-Ghazālī and the philosophers, namely, the application of personal or impersonal analogies to God and the adoption of a monistic or dualistic view of man. In a sense these are basic categories of thought, which are taken for granted throughout civilizations. This is especially true of the second. It is the way in which people think about man throughout a culture, and is perhaps largely determined by which language they use. It is "pre-religious" in the sense that the founder of a religion expresses his new religious message in terms of the categories of thought employed by the people he is addressing. Muḥammad's essential message could presumably have been expressed in terms of a dualistic or of a monistic anthropology; but, since the Arabs already thought monistically, he expressed his message in monistic terms, although the monistic conception of man was not part of his message.

Although categories of thinking such as we have here might be supposed to be objective, there is an element of value about them, and it is proper to examine their social relevance. This is not the place for a full examination of this matter, however, since it would require a wide investigation of the whole earlier history of the Middle East and perhaps further afield. In such an examination the kind of hypothesis to be tested would be, for instance, that the tendency to conceive of ultimate reality as analogous to natural forces is characteristic of agriculturalists, who depend on the regularity of the seasons, whereas the tendency to use personal analogies would be frequent among people like Arabian nomads who find nature irregular and whose tribes prosper or decline according to the quality of the human material. For the conceptions of man a hypothesis worth examining would be that the monistic view of man belonged to people who accepted life and were moderately satisfied with it, whereas the dualistic one found favour rather among those who were, on the whole, dissatisfied.[54a] An alternative would be that the monistic conception corresponded to emphasis on the community, the dualistic to exaggeration of the importance of the individual at the expense of the community.

These particular issues of the eleventh-century caliphate are not altogether dead in the West of our own day. Modern science has emphasized the extent of law in nature, so that we tend to think of ultimate reality as impersonal and find it difficult to fit in the personal, whether in its religious or in its secular form. In our views of man, too, both philosophy and religion, under Greek influence, have propagated a dualistic outlook, but recently modern science, with psychology in the van here, has been moving towards a monistic conception. These contemporary parallels may help us to appreciate the problems confronting al-Ghazālī.

The social context in which the particular categories first appeared is one problem. Another somewhat different problem is that of their transmission to the Muslims of the eleventh century, including both the route of the transmission and the motives governing those who adopted the categories. An important part was played by the conquests of Alexander the Great, which were followed by the spread of Hellenistic culture up to the borders of India. The Islamic philosophy we have been considering was part of this Hellenistic culture, whose tide was now receding. The Qur'ānic categories, again, were taken over by the non-Arab Muslims of the caliphate along with the Islamic religion. They seem to have been whole-heartedly accepted, even although many of the new Muslims had had very different categories previously. This is one of the remarkable features of the situation. In the more strictly religious field, when new ideas are adopted along with a new religion, there tends to be also some recrudescence of old ideas, perhaps after an interval; an example is the idea of the charismatic leader among the Shī'ite Muslims, who give it a prominence unjustified by the Qur'ān. In the case of the monistic view of man, perhaps it was widely accepted because it was assumed or taken for granted rather than explicitly taught—and so slipped in unnoticed—and because it did not obviously thwart any deep religious conviction.

Yet another question worth asking is whether the adoption of the Qur'ānic categories by the non-Arab Muslims has had any independent influence on their outlook and attitudes. To superficial observation Muslims certainly seem to be more conscious than Westerners of the human aspect and to be much less impersonal in their dealings with human beings; but this fact, if it is one, may be due not to these categories of thought, but to their being closer to pre-industrial society.

However fascinating such speculations may be, the primary purpose here is to consider al-Ghazālī's response to the situation in which he found himself, where there was strong tension between two sets of categories. Without hesitation he accepts the Qur'ānic and rejects the philosophical at the various points of conflict which he mentions. He was following his teacher, al-Juwaynī, in adhering to "the religion of the old women". He would not even allow the philosophers to say, as al-Fārābī had said, that the Qur'ānic conceptions were symbolic ones, put forward for the sake of ordinary men who could not comprehend the more abstract language of philosophy.[55] To allow this would have been to allow a certain inferiority to be attached to the Qur'ānic conceptions. If revelation is ultimate, however, reason cannot be permitted to whittle away its supremacy in this fashion. Yet despite this decision al-Ghazālī had been deeply influenced by his philosophical studies. His conception of man (and of the soul) becomes more and more complex as he tries to combine something of both conceptions. In general he was prepared to accept the findings of the "Greek" sciences wherever they did not conflict with religion; for some parts of them, such as the logical doctrine of the syllogism, he became an enthusiast. In the next section we shall consider in detail how much philosophy he was prepared to accept.

5 THE INTRODUCTION OF LOGIC INTO THEOLOGY

The tension which al-Ghazālī found in his environment and into which he entered more fully by a deliberate decision was due to the separation between two disciplines which really belonged together, namely, the Islamic sciences of the scholar-jurists and the "foreign" sciences of the philosophers. As already noted, there had been remarkably little contact between the two sets of intellectuals. The philosophers had fully accepted the existence of the Islamic state, founded by a prophet-statesman, but they had made no allowance in their systems for the fact that in its details the life of the Islamic community depended on a revelation or revealed-law (*sharīʿa*) and that for the proper application of this revelation there had to be a special class of interpreters of it, the scholar-jurists. The philosophers had also made no effort to disseminate their sciences widely. They had had few living contacts with the scholar-jurists, they had presented a subject like logic in an unnecessarily strange technical vocabulary which made it incomprehensible to the average scholar-jurist, and they had strongly suggested that acceptance of any part of their sciences included acceptance of the whole—and this whole included some dubious theological views. The scholar-jurists, for their part, had accepted that amount of Greek philosophy which had been assimilated by the Muʿtazilites in the first half of the ninth century, but had paid no further attention to it. So the two streams had gone their separate ways, and there was now a heritage of suspicion to be overcome.

By the eleventh century the scholar-jurists were realizing that there was much of value in the "foreign" sciences. There are various references to individual scholars reading some of the books of the philosophers,[56] but owing to the widespread popular and scholarly suspicion of the philosophers it was difficult for any scholar-jurist to refer to any philosophical work in his writings. What made it possible for al-Ghazālī to break new ground here was doubtless the support of the Seljūq government for the Ashʿarites and its need for an intellectual defence of the Sunnite position against Shīʿite, especially Ismāʿīlite, propaganda. The extent of the connection between Ismāʿīlism and philosophy is not clear,[57] but a popular belief in such a connection, even if mistaken, would be a sufficient justification for al-Ghazālī to publish his books on *The Aims of the Philosophers* and *The Inconsistency of the Philosophers*.

What in effect al-Ghazālī did was to examine the philosophical sciences to see how much of them was valuable as an addition to the Islamic sciences and how much had to be rejected. As a scholar-jurist he was interested in logical questions, since legal discussions sometimes involved these;[58] and for years he was very enthusiastic about logic. His conclusions about the value of the philosophical sciences as given in *Deliverance from Error*,[59] written about 1108, are the results of his mature reflection. He regards the philosophical sciences as six in number, namely, mathematics, logic, natural science, theology (or metaphysics), politics and ethics.

Mathematics is entirely true, he holds, but the contemporary teaching of it (by the philosophers) is attended by two drawbacks: the students of mathematics tend to think that all the philosophers' arguments are as cogent as their mathematical ones, and ignorant opponents of mathematics from a religious standpoint bring religion in general into disrepute. Logic is likewise true and not contrary to religion in any way, but has the same two drawbacks as mathematics. Natural science or physics need not in general be rejected from the standpoint of religion, but some conclusions of the philosopher-physicists, as enumerated in *The Inconsistency*, are to be rejected. In theology or metaphysics the philosophers differ from one another and have many errors. These fall under twenty heads (as in *The Inconsistency*), of which three constitute unbelief and the rest heresy. (This is not quite correct, since, as was noticed above, some of the seventeen points consist not in false or objectionable doctrines, but in the philosophers' inability to prove rationally points that they claim to prove thus.) Their discussion of politics is merely utilitarian. Their ethics contains sound principles derived from prophets and mystics, together with worthless ideas of their own, and is therefore liable to mislead.

Al-Ghazālī's attitude to the philosophers' ethics is in strong contrast to his attitude to their mathematics, logic and physics. There are traces, however, of a more favourable attitude to philosophical ethics at an earlier period. At the end of an exposition of Aristotelian logic (probably written in 1095) he said he was about to write a complementary work on *The Criterion of Action*.[60] A work with this title has in fact been preserved, some of which is almost certainly genuine, though other parts are definitely not by al-Ghazālī.[61] The genuine part would appear to be an attempt to develop the Aristotelian conception of virtue as a mean, and would clearly be complementary to the logical work. Soon after writing it, however—if indeed he ever completed it to his satisfaction—he must have turned to a complete rejection of the criterion of the mean as a scientific basis for ethics. The condemnation of philosophical ethics in *Deliverance from Error* is paralleled by the absence of references to *The Criterion of Action* in his own later works.[62] Perhaps at the time of his realization that the strict demands of logic were not fulfilled by philosophical theology, he came to see that the same was true of ethics, and in ethics as in theology turned back to the Islamic revelation.

His rejection of ethics makes his extensive writing on logic all the more significant. There are some seventy pages about it in *The Aims of the Philosophers*, two fuller expositions for serious students, a more popular defence of it ostensibly directed against the Bāṭinites, and some slighter references. When this activity of composition is connected with his remarks about the danger of innocent students thinking that all the works of the philosophers were as carefully argued as their logical works, it would seem that he aimed at making available for such students books on logic which were not by philosophers but reached the same standard of technical competence as the philosophers' writings. The provision of an account of the philosophical sciences not by a philosopher may also have been part of his aim in writing *The Aims of the Philosophers*. This would help to explain the curious procedure of writing a separate book about the opponents' views before criticizing them. He thus laid himself open to the charge of disseminating knowledge of heretical views and perhaps misleading the unwary; but he probably felt that it was worth taking this risk in order that students following the normal curriculum might have a chance of learning about logic and physics from a source independent of the philosophers.

The two main logical works, *The Standard for Knowledge* and *The Touchstone of Thinking*, are intended for persons educated in the scholar-jurist tradition. In the first he says he is writing to explain the methods of reasoning and to keep the promise made in *The Inconsistency*. There he had used the technical terms of the philosophers without explanation, since he was writing primarily for philosophers; now he wants to address those not familiar with philosophical books and to show them what the terms mean. The same rules apply to arguments both in philosophical or rational matters (*'aqliyyāt*) and in legal matters (*fiqhiyyāt*); and therefore, to make the subject easier for scholar-jurists, he will take the examples from their field.[63]

While the purpose of these two works is readily understandable, that of *The Just Balance*, the work directed against the Bāṭinites, is obscure. What is puzzling is that much of the work consists in somewhat forced interpretations of Qur'ānic passages to find a justification for the various types of syllogism. A quotation will illustrate his method of procedure:

"The higher criterion is the criterion of Abraham (God bless and preserve him) which he used against Nimrod; from it we learn this criterion, yet by means of the Qur'ān. Nimrod claimed divinity, and divinity for him, as all agree, was an expression for having power over everything. Abraham said, My God is God because he causes to live and to die, and has power over that, and you have no power for that. I do cause to live and to die, he replied, meaning that he caused to live through seed in intercourse and to die through killing. Abraham realized that it was difficult to make him understand the invalidity of this argument, and turned to what would be clearer for him. 'He said, God brings the sun from the east, so do you bring it from the west; the unbeliever was confounded' (2.258/260). God then praised Abraham and said, 'And that proof of ours We gave Abraham against his people' (6. 83). From this I came to see that the proof and demonstration was in what Abraham said and his criterion. I reflected on the manner of his using it, as you might reflect on the criterion of gold and silver. I saw that this proof had two bases, which were married to one another; from the union is born a conclusion, the knowledge gained. For the Qur'ān is founded on omission and compression. The full form of this criterion is to say: 'Everyone who is capable of causing the sun to rise is God—one base'; 'My God is the (one) capable of causing it to rise'—the other base; from the combination of the two it follows that 'My god is God, and not you, Nimrod' ".[64]

The passage concludes with an examination of the source of our knowledge of the premisses.

Now it may be admitted that a syllogism is implicit in the verses of the Qur'ān, but why should it be necessary to argue about it like this? Why should a man like al-Ghazālī, capable of writing a full technical exposition of Aristotelian logic, spend time on trivialities of this kind? Obviously because some people who could not understand the technicalities needed to be assured that logic was based on the Qur'ān. There were many people of this kind until long after al-Ghazālī, even people who rejected geometry.[65] The heart of the problem, however, is why a book against the Bāṭinites should envisage readers of this outlook and level of education, for the Bāṭinites are usually said to have had close connections with certain strands of the philosophical movement. In trying to solve the problem it has to be remembered that the Bāṭinite propaganda had many faces, and tended to become all things to all men. It has also to be remembered that a polemical work may be intended to confirm waverers in one's own ranks rather than to convince the opponents. All that can be done here is to make the general statement that Bāṭinite teaching must have been proving attractive to simple-minded people loyal to the Qur'ān.[66]

The achievement of al-Ghazālī in his encounter with philosophy has left a mark on the whole subsequent course of Islamic thought. He gave theology a philosophical foundation, and also made possible an undue intellectualization of it, though he is not to be blamed if later theologians have gone to excess in their philosophizing. These points will be further considered in the last chapter.

IV

TRUTH FROM THE CHARISMATIC LEADER

INTRODUCTORY NOTE

Of the four groups of people with whom al-Ghazālī had to come to terms, the second to be considered here is the one he calls the Taʿlīmites, the party of "authoritative instruction". This is a section or aspect of the political and religious movement known as Ismāʿīlism; or, to be more precise, al-Ghazālī appears to apply the term Taʿlīmites to those adherents of the Ismāʿīlite movement who laid special emphasis on the doctrine of *taʿlīm* or "authoritative instruction". When he is referring to the movement in a more general way he usually speaks of the Bāṭinites, the people of the *baṭin* or esoteric meaning. The movement has also several other names, but these properly indicate distinct parts of it, since it is a highly complex phenomenon.

IV

TRUTH FROM THE CHARISMATIC LEADER

1 ISMĀʿĪLITE DOCTRINE IN ITS POLITICAL SETTING

WE are fortunate in having a first-hand account of how this movement appeared to an intelligent statesman a year or two before al-Ghazālī wrote his first refutation of it. This is contained in *The Book of Government, or Rules for Kings* by the great vizier Niẓām-al-Mulk (1017–1092), who from 1071 was the virtual ruler of the Seljūq domains. The first and slightly larger half of the book was written about 1086 at the request of the sultan Malikshāh. The second part he added shortly before his death, and more than half of this part is devoted to the Bāṭinite heretics and revolutionaries, and their antecedents. This is evidence of increasing anxiety over the Bāṭinite movement, perhaps owing to the success of the armed rising which resulted in the capture of Alamūt in 1090. The interesting point about Niẓām-al-Mulk's account is that he regards as Bāṭinite or approximately Bāṭinite a number of revolts in various parts of the east between 750 and 975, and even the pre-Islamic Mazdakite movement which was suppressed by the Sasanian ruler of the Persian empire about 530. It is worth pausing for a moment to ask whether there is justification in regarding these earlier movements as forerunners of the Bāṭinism of the late eleventh century.

Niẓām-al-Mulk would probably have justified his view by showing that all these movements were revolts against established authority in the interests of a different kind of authority, that they were supported by discontented groups among the ordinary people and led by courtiers and administrators, and that they were hostile to the Sunnite scholar-jurists and therefore to the principles of law and social morality on which the Islamic state was based. He would probably have admitted that there was no absolute identity of doctrine among them and practically no direct influence of one on another. Yet from his standpoint of a politician not interested in theological niceties there was a substantial identity, especially in the fact that "the constant object of them all is to overthrow Islam".[1] It would hardly be too much to say that this was a political movement masquerading as a religious and philosophical one. In other words, though there were Ismā'īlite doctrines, the leaders of the movement do not seem to have been committed to any definite doctrines, but rather to have manipulated the doctrines to serve their political ends. Yet another way of putting this would be to say that the movement had no fixed ideational basis, but that the supreme leader had control of the ideational basis and could modify it as he thought fit.

The control of the thinking of the movement by the imam or supreme leader was strengthened by the organization of the movement in a series of grades.[2] Only a limited amount of truth was given to the lower grades, and that might be adapted to the existing outlook of a person or local group. Thus to Muslims of different sects and even to non-Muslims such as Zoroastrians, Bāṭinism could be made to seem not very different from what they already believed, and indeed a fulfilment of it. Where there were discontented Sunnites, or Sunnites under Ismā'īlite rule (as in Egypt), the lowest grade was not far from Sunnite Islam, and care was taken to make a show of deriving Ismā'īlite teaching from the Qur'ān. It is doubtless because many of the common people who were adherents of Bāṭinism or likely to be influenced by it were also deeply attached to the Qur'ān that al-Ghazālī (as noted at the end of the previous chapter) in writing *The Just Balance* against the Bāṭinites had to claim that logical theory was derived from the Qur'ān. Those initiated into the higher grades of the movement, however—at least in some periods and in some parts of the Islamic world—held philosophical views about the equivalence of all religions which practically placed them outside the community of Muslims. To what extent these leaders seriously considered abandoning the Islamic community (or should we say "abandoning an Islamic basis for the community"?) we shall probably never know for certain. They were undoubtedly hostile to Islam as Niẓām-al-Mulk conceived it, and in their doctrines they had an instrument that could be used for its destruction.

The flexibility in propaganda was something which had developed gradually. Originally there had been a definite ideational basis, since Ismā'īlism was a branch of Shī'ism and had much in common with the other branches. While it has sometimes been held that the earliest Shī'ites were Arabs who supported 'Alī for political reasons, careful study of the sources suggests that from the first some of the followers of 'Alī were seeking in him an embodiment of the archetype or dynamic image of the charismatic leader.[3] A survey of the whole history of Shī'ism further suggests that, though it has had political implications, it has always been primarily a religious movement, and that its purely political ideas have never been sufficiently good as political ideas to arouse the devotion that has been manifested. Politically it has stood for autocracy, perhaps at times for a benevolent autocracy giving full consideration to the interests of the lower classes; and for some adherents this political appeal may have been uppermost. Essentially, however, what the various branches of Shīʿism have in common is not the political principle of autocracy but the fundamentally religious quest for the charismatic leader. Some of the phenomena where politics seem to predominate are to be interpreted as the attempts of politicians, whether sincere or unscrupulous, to make use for their political ends of this deep religious yearning.

The Ismāʿīlite branch of Shīʿism seems to have separated from the main body about 765. It receives its name from recognizing as imam the previous imam's son Ismāʿīl instead of another son Mūsā who was recognized by the main body. For the next century and a half the history is obscure, and there are important disagreements among historians. It became more associated with revolutionary bodies and ideas than other branches of Shīʿism. Shortly before 900 there was a resurgence of Ismāʿīlism, as a result of which an Ismāʿīlite dynasty known as the Fāṭimids was established in Tunisia in 909. In 969 this dynasty conquered Egypt, and shortly afterwards founded Cairo as their capital. Because of their Ismāʿīlite conception of the imam of the Muslim community the Fāṭimids, unlike other powerful provincial dynasties, did not recognize the nominal suzerainty of the ʿAbbāsid caliphs. On the contrary, they themselves claimed to be the rightful caliphs of the whole Islamic world, and they organized a propaganda machine (*daʿwa*) and sent agents (sing. *dāʿī*) throughout the ʿAbbāsid domains to disseminate their teachings and make contact with discontented and dissident groups.

Because of the flexibility already noted the Fāṭimid agents were very successful in making contacts and gaining adherents. Possibly the reason for Niẓām-al-Mulk not mentioning any revolts after 975 is that any subsequent revolts were so clearly connected with the Fāṭimids that no one would imagine they were separate.

One of the important groups which acknowledged the Fāṭimid rulers as imams were the Qarmaṭians or Carmathians of Bahrein, who ruled a small state on the Persian Gulf.[4] The Brethren of Purity (Ikhwān aṣ-Ṣafā') in Basra, a coterie of philosophers and natural scientists with Neopythagorean leanings, also gave some degree of allegiance to the Fāṭimids and probably made an important contribution to the ideational basis.[5]

This is, of course, not a complete account of the successes of the Fāṭimid propagandists in the 'Abbāsid caliphate, but only an indication of the complexity of the story. Another aspect of this complexity is revealed in the attempt to discover the identity of the supporters of the movement. It is commonly held that the Ismā'īlites were the political party of the labouring and artisan class in their struggle against the upper class.[6] There is probably much truth in this view, but it is not easy to square it with some important materials. It could perhaps be said to be implicit in Niẓām-al-Mulk's account of the Bāṭinites, but he only speaks of leaders who are courtiers and administrators. In the *Mustaẓ'hirī*, the book dedicated to the caliph al-Mustaẓ'hir, al-Ghazālī speaks of eight classes of persons who are attracted by the movement:[7] (1) people with a tendency to deify men (such as 'Alī); (2) Persian nationalists seeking to recover autonomy; (3) men seeking power or vengeance; (4) people who think themselves superior to the masses and seek something strange and unusual; (5) superficial and dilettante members of philosophical coteries; (6) atheistic philosophers and dualists; (7) people of Shī'ite tendencies who are sympathetic to Bāṭinite teaching; (8) men dominated by their passions who find the religious law irksome. Now some of these categories might include labourers and artisans, but several exclude these. The Brethren of Purity come in the sixth group, and some perhaps also in the fifth. The explanation and expansion of all these statements would require a long investigation; but even without expansion they illustrate the complexity of the movement.

In the troubled years after the fall of the Buwayhid dynasty of Baghdad in 1055 the Fāṭimids achieved their most successful penetration of the ʿAbbāsid realm. A Turkish general was won over to their cause after the fall of his Buwayhid masters, and was able to occupy Baghdad in their name for nearly a year, so that it was they and not the ʿAbbāsids who were mentioned in the Friday prayers.[8] By about 1060, however, the Seljūq sultan had so consolidated his power with Baghdad as capital that there was little likelihood of a successful pro-Fāṭimid revolution. Egypt began to suffer from internal troubles. The later leader of the Ismāʿīlite movement in Persia, al-Ḥasan ibn-aṣ-Ṣabbāḥ, visited Egypt in 1078. Whether or not he was badly treated by one faction, as is sometimes stated, he must have seen for himself that the Fāṭimid government was losing its revolutionary fervour and, besides having little enthusiasm, was no longer capable of making an effective intervention in the east. On his return to Persia he spent several years travelling about and organized a revolt that did not count on Fāṭimid help. By 1090 he was able to seize the fortress of Alamūt in southern Persia; and on October 14, 1092, one of his followers assassinated Niẓām-al-Mulk—one of the first instances of this activity which gets its English name from a nickname of these Ismāʿīlites, "hashish-men", *ḥashshāshīn*, corrupted to Assassins.

It is primarily of these Persian (Khurasanian) Ismāʿīlites that al-Ghazālī is thinking when he speaks of Taʿlīmites, for his usual phrase is "the Bāṭinites of our time"; and in other sources al-Ḥasan is credited with being the author of the "new teaching" which emphasized *taʿlīm* or authoritative instruction.[9] (The subsequent doctrinal developments of this branch of Ismā'īlism, beginning with their adoption of Nizār as "hidden imam",[10] do not concern a study of al-Ghazālī, since they do not appear to have come to the knowledge of the Sunnite world during his lifetime.) The doctrine of authoritative instruction, namely, that in order to learn the truth about anything you have to ask, and be instructed by, the infallible imam, is an understandable development of earlier Shī'ism. The Fāṭimids also had the principle (if reliance can be placed on a later document),[11] but probably placed less emphasis on it.

The essence of Shī'ism is belief in the imam or charismatic leader, which includes the belief that salvation, or keeping to the straight path and avoiding error, comes from following the imam, in contrast to the Sunnite belief that it comes from being a member of the charismatic community. In keeping with the essential belief, the imam came to be regarded as a source of truth or guidance for his followers. This point was involved in the theological discussions in the ninth century about the createdness of the Qur'ān. By holding that the Qur'ān was the eternal and uncreated Word of God men were insisting that the source of the "beaten path" (*sunna*) or, as we might say, the "way of life" of the community was supernatural, and were thereby justifying Sunnite claims for the community. The Mu'tazilite and other upholders of the opposing view that the Qur'ān was created were interested in placing more emphasis on the charismatic leader, that is, in political terms, in increasing the powers of the ruler and his advisers and in decreasing those of the scholar-jurists, the official exponents of the system of law based on Qur'ānic principles as expanded in Tradition.

Some Ismā'īlite formulations speak of a parallelism of the imam and the Qur'ān;[12] but to the detached student this seems to be a sop to the Sunnite feelings of the masses. The doctrine of authoritative instruction had as its complement the conception of the "esoteric meaning" (*bāṭin*). By this everything in the Qur'ān (and in the Traditions and religious institutions) had an esoteric meaning, which bore no necessary resemblance to its plain or exoteric meaning, and which could only be learnt from the imam. Thus heaven and hell could be particular men. In this way it was possible to continue to pay lip-service to the Qur'ān, and yet to ensure that the Qur'ān placed not the slightest check on the imam's control of the ideational basis of the community and therefore of its whole life. Al-Ḥasan ibn-aṣ-Ṣabbāḥ seems to have greatly increased the emphasis on this aspect of Ismā'īlite teaching by insisting that truth could *only* be learned from the imam. Personal effort (*ijtihād*) in thinking and reasoning (*ra'y*, *naẓar*), he argued, could not lead to truth, since their exponents were always in disagreement. This was a direct attack on the scholar-jurists. The promise of unity, too, must have had a strong appeal for men who remembered the period of anarchy prior to the Seljūq conquest, and probably looked on political and ideational disunity as the cause of their sufferings.[13]

The nature of Ismā'īlism may best be summarized by considering the relations between the ruler or government and the intellectuals (the bearers of the ideational foundation of a movement). In Sunnite Islam in its classical form the ruler had no control at all over the ideational basis; he could not even legislate in the strict sense, since all possible legislation was in principle contained in the Qur'ān and Traditions, and of these the intellectuals, the scholar-jurists, were the guardians. In the Russian form of Marxism the ruler (Lenin, Stalin, Khrushchev) has become the controller of the ideational basis of the state, since only he can give the "correct" interpretation of Marxist doctrine to meet the needs of the contemporary situation.[13a] His control of ideation, however, is limited by the existence of a corpus of documents—the works of Marx, Engels and Lenin. In Ismā'īlism even this last limitation has been removed. Though there is a corpus of documents which has been acknowledged, its efficacy as a check on the ruler has been destroyed by the conception of the esoteric meaning. Thus the Ismā'īlism of the Assassins stands for complete autocracy, in which the whole life of the community is derived from the ruler in much the same way as all existence emanates from the Neoplatonic One.

2 THE INTELLECTUAL DEFENCE OF SUNNISM

Al-Ghazālī's outlook was close to that of Niẓām-al-Mulk. This may be presumed from his association with the statesman, but it is also shown by passages in his writings, such as his repetition of the dictum that "religion and government are twin-brothers".[14] He must also have shared the older man's concern about the growth of Ismā'īlism, and that concern would not have been lessened by Niẓām-al-Mulk's assassination in 1092. He therefore responded with alacrity to the request of the young caliph al-Mustaẓ'hir that he should write a book in refutation of the doctrines of the Ta'līmites or Bāṭinites. Al-Mustaẓ'hir came to the throne on February 7, 1094, and the book was completed before al-Ghazālī left Baghdad in November 1095; it was probably written during 1095.[15] This book is commonly known as the *Mustaẓ'hirī*. Al-Ghazālī subsequently wrote several other works directed in whole or in part against the Bāṭinites. *The Just Balance*, as already noted, justifies logical principles by reference to the Qur'ān, and must have been intended for relatively simple-minded believers. A manuscript of one of the shorter works has been discovered recently,[16] but the remainder seem to have perished.

By including the Taʿlīmites among the four groups of seekers whose works he studies in his quest for truth (according to the account in *Deliverance from Error*), al-Ghazālī suggests that the doctrine had some attraction for him. This suggestion is not to be pressed, however. *Deliverance from Error*, as has already been seen, is not a strict autobiography. On general grounds it seems unlikely that he was ever seriously attracted by the idea of authoritative instruction. The whole Bāṭinite movement was bitterly hostile to the class of scholar-jurists to which he belonged (even if he also was critical of the class). His skill in logic, too, must soon have shown him the weakness of the Taʿlīmite position. His chief aim in studying Taʿlīmite doctrine seems to have been to try to appreciate what it was in it which attracted men.

It is perhaps appropriate also at this point to notice the suggestion that fear of the Bāṭinites and of assassination was the main motive of al-Ghazālī's actions at this time.[17] This suggestion, too, is to be rejected. Since he had been prominent as an opponent of the Bāṭinites, he may have had some fear of assassination; but it is almost certain that assassination had not come to be thought characteristic of the Assassins in the Baghdad of 1095, since most of the instances are later. Moreover, al-Ghazālī says that it was hell he was afraid of, not death.[18] That indicates a sense that something was wrong with the quality of his life. To be murdered by a Bāṭinite, on the other hand, would have been regarded by him as martyrdom and tending to ensure entrance to paradise. So the arguments against the suggestion are strong; and in the following chapters it will be shown that there is a satisfying alternative explanation.

In the *Mustaẓʾhirī* al-Ghazālī places considerable

emphasis on the doctrine of authoritative instruction and its complements—over thirty folios out of just over a hundred—and in *Deliverance from Error* it is the main topic to be discussed in connection with the Taʿlīmites. The emphasis is justified by the prominence given to the doctrine in the "new teaching" of al-Ḥasan ibn-aṣ-Ṣabbāḥ. About the time the caliph asked him to write on this subject, too, he had been very interested in logic, and had been studying it hard and writing about it. He doubtless felt that this was a field in which he could easily defeat his opponents, and perhaps impress their philosophically-minded adherents. Most polemic, of course, though ostensibly directed against opponents, is really intended to give support to members of one's own party who are in danger of being convinced by the opponent's arguments. Al-Ghazālī's argumentation here would fit in well with this conception. It shows that, though they profess to abandon reasoning, they cannot avoid surreptitiously making use of it, and that it is practically impossible to consult the imam or his representative in every case; he does not attack their esoteric doctrines. In other words, a large part of al-Ghazālī's intellectual effort is to show the inconsistencies of the Taʿlīmites.

There is an important difference between the *Mustaẓhirī* and *Deliverance from Error*. The former, being commissioned by the caliph, naturally has a section proving that he and not the Fāṭimid ruler in Cairo is the rightful caliph. This is along the usual juristic lines, and in accordance with the utilitarian conception of the imamate held by al-Ghazālī.[19] By about 1108, however, when he wrote *Deliverance from Error*, he had a deeper appreciation of what lay behind the Bāṭinite movement. He was no longer content with destructive criticism of his opponents, but had realized that part of their success was due to the fact that they satisfied, however imperfectly, the deep demand in men's hearts for an embodiment of the dynamic image of the charismatic leader. So he now insists that Muslims have such a leader, but that he is Muḥammad. He has his living expositors (presumably the scholar-jurists are meant), just as the hidden imam has his expositors, the accredited agents. In a sense he is thus carrying the war into the enemy's camp. Yet he has not altogether met the deep need in men's hearts. To put it in Islamic language, there is always a hope that a hidden imam may reappear, but there is no hope of the return of Muḥammad before the Last Day. In other words, the desire for a leader is not fully satisfied. In so far as that is a desire for a leader who is active in the present or who may be active in the not-too-distant future it is not satisfied. Is it the failure of Sunnism to satisfy such a desire that has prevented the reunion of Sunnism and Shī'ism?

It is perhaps worth calling attention here to what al-Ghazālī does not say. Though the 'Abbāsid caliphs had originally claimed to have charismata, he does not attempt to make them into imams of the Bāṭinite type. Their position, now shorn of nearly all real power, would have made this ludicrous. Neither does he attempt to attribute any charismata to the scholar-jurists, apart from the vague phrase about the expositors or preachers of Muḥammad's message, which does not necessarily refer to them alone or even to them at all. Had he wanted he could have referred to the Tradition that the scholar-jurists were the heirs of the prophets, but he took such a low view of the condition of the scholar-jurists in his own day that he understandably passed them over. His later thought, as we shall see, tended to the view that there was an elite who, by treading the path of the mystics or ṣūfīs, could obtain an insight into divine truth comparable to that of the prophets. It is perhaps in parts of his later works apparently unconnected with contemporary problems that we find his real and effective answer to the challenge of Ismāʿīlism, which, even if it had little effect on the ruling institution, enabled Islamic society to preserve its characteristic structure and manner of life.

V
THE REAPPRAISAL OF THEOLOGY

INTRODUCTORY NOTE

Al-Ghazālī was by training a jurist and a theologian, and his attitude to these disciplines must be taken to have had a central place in his development. There is a tendency among Western scholars to regard Islamic theology as trivial hair-splitting, and therefore to suppose that in his later period al-Ghazālī felt the same distaste for it that they feel. This is a complete failure to appreciate what theology meant to him and to men in a similar position.

The standpoint of this book may be roughly described as that of the sociology of knowledge. The theologian is looked upon as a type of intellectual with an important function to perform in the community. Firstly, it is his business to formulate the objectives of the community and the view of the nature of reality (including values) associated with these objectives. Secondly, he has to systematize this ideational basis of the community by smoothing out discrepancies which lead to tensions, either discrepancies originally present or those due to novel circumstances; that is to say, in systematizing the ideational basis of the community he is also adapting it to external changes affecting the community. If we are to understand the place of al-Ghazālī in Islamic theology, we must have some idea of what had been achieved by earlier theologians.

V

THE REAPPRAISAL OF THEOLOGY

I THE ACHIEVEMENTS OF ISLAMIC THEOLOGY

THE first theological developments in Islam came after the first wave of conquest had subsided. When the excitement of advance was over, discontent began to appear, probably mainly due to the feeling of insecurity consequent upon the revolutionary changes in the way of life of the Arabs who formed the Muslim armies. This discontent led to the assassination of the caliph ʿUthmān in 656. In the disturbed conditions of the following period, when ʿAlī was caliph but not universally recognized, there appeared the two contrasting sects of the Khārijites and the Shīʿites.

The essential feature of the Khārijites was their emphasis on the dynamic idea or image of the charismatic community,[1] an idea which was implicit in the Qur'ān and in the life of the Muslim state. Originally, however, the Khārijites adopted this idea in an unsuitable form. Anyone, they said, who committed a grave sin, would be punished in Hell, and so belonged to the people of Hell; he was no longer a believer or member of the Islamic community, and thus there was no sin in killing him. In practice this meant that small groups of Khārijites, regarding themselves as "saints" and all other men as enemies, revolted against the government (which consisted in their eyes of "grave sinners"). One of the important achievements of the theologians, especially those in Basra in the last half-century of Umayyad rule, was to transform this dynamic idea so that it became applicable to the whole body of Muslims, scattered over what was now a world empire. They made it possible for Muslims to regard themselves as belonging to a community that was divinely constituted (and brought important advantages to its members), yet which did not lose this character through the sins of some members.

Meanwhile another group of people, the Shīʿites, living in the same conditions, tried to find security by emphasizing the dynamic image of the charismatic leader—the divinely-sent and divinely-inspired leader who could guide them to safety through the perils of the world.[2] There was not much in the Qur'ān about such a charismatic leader, but Muḥammad himself was clearly one. The idea that was developed, then, was that other members of his family shared in his divinely-conferred qualities. Though later Shīʿites came to regard such charismata as belonging only to descendants of Muḥammad's cousin and daughter, ʿAlī and Fāṭima, in the Umayyad period some men were prepared to allow that the whole clan of Hāshim shared in the charismata. The ʿAbbāsid family made claims embodying this conception, namely, that they were the heirs of the charismata, and many no doubt believed their claims; but there were also many still dissatisfied. The numbers and importance of Shīʿites and Shīʿite-sympathizers during the first century of ʿAbbāsid rule (750–850) is a problem that has not been adequately studied. The two theological tendencies just described, the Shīʿite and what eventually became the Sunnite, appear to be linked up with political factors, which I have tried to indicate provisionally by speaking of the "autocratic" and "constitutionalist" blocs.[3] This contrast and opposition will appear repeatedly in the following pages.

The Umayyad period is also noteworthy for raising the problem of human freedom or responsibility and divine omnipotence or predestination. This again had a political reference. Is a man bound to accept an unjust government (such as many held the Umayyad dynasty to be), or is he *free* to rebel against it? For the Khārijites this problem was linked with their conception of the nature of the community; could the community be a charismatic one if the ruler was a wrongdoer? The discussion continued well into the 'Abbāsid period, by which time the political situation was entirely different. The outstanding protagonists of human freedom were the Mu'tazilites, who had adopted something of the Greek intellectual outlook, and who linked the question of man's freedom with that of God's justice. In the end the great majority of Muslims, however, firmly asserted God's omnipotence. They allowed that man was free, to a sufficient extent for him to be justly punished for his acts on the Last Day, but in general they thought that he determined events only within narrow limits and then subject to God's will. Perhaps they felt that there was something inevitable about the Islamic state, or perhaps they merely realized the limitations of human planning. However that may be, the result was the general acceptance by Muslims of this element from their Arabian heritage—the sense that life is determined by forces beyond man's control—and a general rejection of the Greek conception of freedom.

By about 800 the conception of the Sunna had taken shape, and many Muslims were speaking of themselves as "the people of the Sunna". The Sunna may be described as the divinely-appointed way of life or mores of the community. The conception developed out of legal discussions about what was right or wrong according to Islamic principles with regard to certain points. For a time men were content to say that "the view of our school is so-and-so" or "the view of N (an important member of the school) was so-and-so". The practice grew up, however, of supporting particular legal views by anecdotes about something that Muḥammad had said or done, such anecdotes being technically known as Traditions and being accompanied by an *isnād* or list of transmitters. After the work of ash-Shāfi'ī (d. 820) Traditions became the normal vehicle for legal and other views. Where there was no Tradition or only an anecdote with an imperfect *isnād*, it became necessary to complete the *isnād*, to modify an existing Tradition, or even to invent a new one. All the inherited wisdom of the Middle East, one might almost say, came to be incorporated in Traditions. Muslim scholars realized that many Traditions were spurious, and had elaborate rules for the critique of Traditions; but the aim of this critique was not the establishing of objective truth in a modern sense, but, as noted above (p. 10), the elimination of the eccentric views of the "lunatic fringe" and the retention of views acceptable to the main body of Muslims. This aim was more or less realized.[4]

The conception that thus emerged was that of the Sunna (or "beaten path") of the Prophet, and this was taken to be a form of revelation, roughly on a level with the Qur'ān itself. This strengthened the belief that the Islamic community was a charismatic one, since it had a fixed way of life that was God-inspired and God-given. To the modern observer there may appear to be an element of "ideology" or distortion in this conception. The Arab contribution to Islamic culture is greatly exaggerated and that of other peoples neglected. Even if allowance is made for the mysterious way in which the Arab element has moulded the whole, there is still exaggeration; and this exaggeration of the Arab contribution helps us to understand the protest against Arab superiority in the Shu'ūbite movement.[5]

There was one part of the inherited culture of the Middle East which could not be incorporated into Traditions, and that was philosophy or, to describe it more accurately, the "scientific world-view" of the time.

Besides the philosophical movement within Islam which has been discussed above (in chapter III) there was in certain Traditionist circles an interest in philosophical or rational theology, mostly called *kalām* (and its practitioners *mutakallimūn*). This perhaps began about 780. The men who engaged in the new discipline had different views on various theological questions, but gradually some of the more outstanding became marked off from the rest not merely by the adoption of rational methods of argument but also by agreeing about certain dogmatic positions. This group called themselves the Muʿtazila, and many Western scholars, especially in the nineteenth century, found them the most congenial of Islamic theological schools. As was seen above, they stood for free will against predestination. They are also noted for insisting that the Qur'ān was created. These two points are sufficient to show that the Muʿtazilites had adopted not merely Greek methods of rational argument but also certain Greek conceptions. Indeed, in more ways than can be mentioned here they were trying to effect some reconciliation between revelation and reason. This was a political matter, however, as well as an intellectual one. Reason and philosophy, we saw, tended to be associated with the class of secretaries and administrators. Revelation, on the other hand, had an obvious connection with the rising class of Islamic intellectuals, the scholar-jurists or ulema, which was being formed out of what under the Umayyads had been the "pious opposition" and what later became the Traditionist movement. This latter class was the bearer of the conception of the Sunna, both in general and in detail, and naturally wanted the community to be based exclusively on the Qur'ān and the Sunna. They were the main members of what has been called the "constitutionalist bloc". Though the Muʿtazilites arose out of this class of Islamic intellectuals their main aim seems to have been to achieve a wide synthesis or compromise, and some of them had distinct Shīʿite sympathies. Shīʿ-ism is linked with reason and the "autocratic bloc". It has been noticed how the philosophy of al-Fārābī lends itself to be the justification of a thoroughgoing autocracy, in which the court and the administration are the creatures of the ruler. This autocratic trend is in accordance with a deep political tradition in the Middle East, but it seems to be provoked above all by a religious need—the need for an embodiment of the archetype or dynamic image of the charismatic leader. Man wanted to feel that he was being guided through the troubles of the world by a leader with supernatural gifts. The difficulty, however, was that none of the leaders actually acclaimed as having supernatural powers was much of a success politically. Even the Fāṭimid dynasty in Egypt, though its rule lasted in all for over two centuries, produced no politically impressive results.

In this situation it is to be counted another of the achievements of the theologians that the main body of Muslims rejected the Muʿtazilite view that the Qur'ān was created and instead asserted as a dogma that it was the very Word or Speech of God and uncreated. This is not mere hair-splitting, for it is a reinforcement of the view that the Islamic community is divinely constituted, that is, that it has been given a definite form of life by God. The Qur'ān, the basic scripture of the community, contains the verbal description of this form of life, and also expresses simply and concretely the value-beliefs that are presupposed by this form of life and the associated and equally presupposed views about the ultimate nature of reality. This point will concern us further in the next section, for the Muʿtazilite doctrine of the createdness of the Qur'ān was the basis of the Miḥna or Inquisition (833–849), which was an important event in the relationships of the scholar-jurists to the rulers.

The discussions about the Qur'ān led on to wider-ranging discussions about the attributes of God. In the Qur'ān many epithets were given to God, such as "merciful", "forgiving", "knowing". The question was raised whether God had attributes of "mercy" and "knowledge" which were somehow distinct from his essence. Those who held that the Qur'ān was uncreated tended to say that it was the Speech of God, and that therefore God had an attribute of speech which, though an integral part of him, was also in some way distinct. Seven attributes came to be recognized as essential: life, knowledge (omniscience), power (omnipotence), will, hearing, seeing, speech. The Muʿtazilites, on the other hand, while bound to accept the Qur'ānic epithets as epithets, denied that God had any attributes distinct from his essence. Thus, where he knew, he did so by his essence and not by a separate attribute of knowledge. It is difficult for the modern student to understand what is at stake here. Perhaps it is merely a defence of the supernatural character of the Qur'ān as the Speech of God by insisting that there are other attributes which are also in some sense distinct from his essence. Perhaps it is also intended to reinforce the belief that God is not a bare unity, as reason tends to conceive him, but that God or ultimate reality has a determinate character known by revelation; in this it would be implied that this understanding of ultimate reality is constitutive of the community.

Parallel with the discussions about God's attributes (and the continuation of the debates on other questions at issue between the Muʿtazilites and the Sunnites) there was a movement, among those who held the usual Sunnite position, for the acceptance of rational methods of argument. The important figure is al-Ashʿarī (d. 935), who was trained as a Muʿtazilite but in 912 at the age of forty abandoned Muʿtazilism for the Sunnism of the

Traditionist movement; at the same time, however, he defended, by the methods of the Muʿtazilites, the doctrines he had come to hold, and thus inaugurated one of the main schools of Islamic theology, the Ashʿarite. Another similar school was growing up in the east about the same time, the Māturīdite. A large section of the Traditionist movement still held aloof and continued to avoid "rational" theology; and this section eventually became almost identical with the adherents of the Ḥanbalite legal rite, and may therefore conveniently be referred to as Ḥanbalites. The formation of these theological schools (the Ashʿarite and Māturīdite) marks a stage in the incorporation of the "scientific world-view" of the time into Islamic thought. It was still only a partial incorporation, for it was largely dependent on what had been assimilated by the Muʿtazilites in the time of al-Ma'mūn (813–833). After that period the scholar-jurists had probably little access to Greek thought, for it was studied almost solely by non-Muslims or in little secluded coteries (as was seen in chapter III). So what was achieved, though important, was far from complete.

In the period between al-Ashʿarī and al-Ghazālī the Ashʿarite and Māturīdite schools of theology perfected their techniques (while remaining on the same plane, as it were) and extended them to the whole field of theological discussion. There were certain changes in emphasis, and some new points came to the fore, such as the distinction between miracle and magic. It was only with al-Ghazālī, however, as we have seen, that the advances in philosophy since al-Ma'mūn were taken into account by a theologian, so that it became possible for theology to rise to a higher technical plane. While this point about the relation of theology to Greek thought is tolerably clear, it is not clear whether the theologians had succeeded in maintaining a living relation between theology and the contemporary historical and political situation, where the caliph had lost most of his power and retained only a nominal suzerainty. At the moment this question need only be suggested, since it is more appropriate to discuss it later.

Among minor achievements of the theologians in the period up to 950 were the defence of Islam against various non-Muslim groups within the borders of the state. The Muʿtazilites are known as upholders of Islam against the Manichaeanism found in the secretary class and elsewhere, and also against Jews and Christians. In the case of the latter the aim seems to have been to stop ordinary Muslims from arguing with "the people of the Book". This was secured by the doctrine of the "corruption" (*taḥrīf*) of the Jewish and Christian scriptures —the Bible; but it is noteworthy that the doctrine was never precisely formulated. In its amoeba-like changes of form it served its end, for, if a Muslim found one form of the doctrine did not suit a particular argument, he could always shift to another.[6]

As a whole these achievements of the theologians may be described as the formulation of dogma; and a little reflection on the course of thought just described will lead to a better understanding of the place of dogma in the life of a society. In many of the great disputes the question at issue was whether the life of this great community was to be governed by Muḥammad's vision of the nature of human life and of the universe in which it has to be lived, or by some other. In their details, however, the struggles seem to be remote from this, and to be waged round unimportant abstractions. What does it matter to a great empire, one asks, whether the Qur'ān is created or uncreated? The answer is that this point in itself perhaps does not matter, but that something is involved in it which does matter. A study of polemics, whether political, religious or any other, shows that the points at which battle is joined are not necessarily the most important, but those at which an attacking side thinks it has advantageous ground or a defending side thinks it can yield no further without suffering complete defeat.

In the particular case mentioned, those who objected to the importance attached to the Qur'ān (and the Traditions) in the life of the community doubtless thought that, in asserting the Qur'ān was created, they had a good point. The Qur'ān had manifestly appeared at a certain moment (or rather series of moments) in time, and by insisting on this they no doubt hoped to weaken the case of those who thought that Qur'ānic principles should control the life of the state. The other side, however, feeling strongly that the Qur'ān was the supernatural basis of the community (and knowing that for some of them their material livelihood was bound up with the general acceptance of this point), decided to stand firm here and to insist that the Qur'ān as God's speech was uncreated. The question had all sorts of ramifications. The opponents could reply, "If you repeat the Qur'ān, the sounds you make are not eternal; if it is written, the paper and ink are not eternal". This objection could be met by making further distinctions, and these would lead to further questions. Eventually, however, one side gets the better of the argument. The vast majority go to this side, and the other side is left as a dwindling minority. The majority formulates succinctly the point for which they have been fighting, and it becomes a dogma. A dogma is thus an assertion which after long argument is accepted by the main body of the community and which is felt to safeguard something essential to the well-being of the community.

Dogma is the record of an agreement. The community does not want to repeat the argument, at least not for a long time. Theoretically the possibility of reopening the question cannot be excluded, but in practice it is not contemplated. Indeed, one might doubt whether Islam would remain Islam if it changed its mind about the uncreatedness of the Qur'ān. Thus the assertion about which agreement is reached is given a special status, and comes to have a measure of fixity. This fixity gives stability to the life of the community. Provided there has been adequate discussion before the dogma has been formulated, and provided political pressure has not been used to gain the acceptance of a formula not sincerely accepted by the majority, this fixity is most valuable. The great civilizations of the past have nearly always had the security that comes from a relatively fixed and stable ideational basis.

On the other hand, fixity can be bad if it prevents adjustment of the ideational basis of the community to changing circumstances. Much of the bad odour attached to "dogma" at the present time is due to the fact that our Western Christian dogmas have been too rigid to be easily modified to meet the bewilderingly rapid changes in our circumstances. It must be noticed here, however, that the failure to become adapted to new situations may not be due to faults in the dogmas themselves, for it is usually possible to effect some refinement in the conceptions. Most often the difficulty is that the bearers of the dogmas feel that their privileged status is being threatened and so are unwilling to make the modifications. Whether something of this sort had happened to the Muslim intellectuals before al-Ghazālī is an important question that will have to be considered.

2 THEOLOGIANS AND GOVERNMENTS

To consider, as has just been done, the contemporary relevance of the ideas of the theologians is not in itself sufficient. It is also necessary, for an understanding of al-Ghazālī's position, to look at the relations of the ruling institution or government to the theologians, and more generally to the whole class of religious intellectuals. Here again we stumble into a field which has not been much cultivated by scholars; but from little patches here and there we obtain what we hope is a reliable sample of the yield of the whole area.

During the Umayyad period the class of religious intellectuals was only in process of formation. In a few centres, such as Medina and Basra, devout men began to discuss questions which presented themselves in the course of their practice of the Islamic religion. At first, questions of conduct probably occupied most attention, either the conduct of the rulers towards those whom they ruled or the conduct of individual Muslims towards one another. Gradually some of these questions were found to involve more strictly theological points; but even at the end of the Umayyad period it could hardly be said that a "systematic" theology had been formulated. The earliest theological views were those of opponents of the government, Khārijites and Shī'ites, but in the course of time theological positions were worked out, notably that of the Murji'ites, which would most naturally be associated with support of the Umayyad regime. The body of men, mainly in Medina, who were interested in matters of conduct and an Islamic way of life, are sometimes called the "pious opposition" because, though not active opponents of the Umayyads, they disapproved of their Arab rather than Islamic outlook. It further appears that this "pious opposition" gave its general support to the movement which brought about the replacement of the Umayyads by the 'Abbāsids, and that the 'Abbāsids in return gave some recognition to the "Islamic law" which the devout scholars were in process of elaborating. Among other things this recognition meant the appointment of judges by the government from among the devout scholars.[7]

This understanding between the government and the religious intellectuals was in keeping with the Persian political tradition which the ʿAbbāsids followed to a great extent. There was a Persian saying that "religion and government are twin-brothers",[8] and under the Sasanian empire the Zoroastrian clergy had become almost a department of government. It is therefore not surprising that soon after their coming to power in 750 the ʿAbbāsids are found persecuting the holders of religio-political views of which they disapproved. There was a persecution of *zindīqs* from about 779 to 786,[9] and we hear of persons of Shīʿite sympathies being imprisoned during the reign of ar-Rashīd (786–809).[10] Even under the Umayyads there had been some use of force against religious sectaries, but the main reason seems to have been political rather than theological.[11] For the ʿAbbāsid persecutions just mentioned there may have been political reasons; for example, many of those executed or imprisoned as *zindīqs* belonged to the secretary class which was opposed to the growing power of the Muslim religious intellectuals. Yet there was also a tendency to regard a man's theological views, apart from any obvious political reference, as a matter of which the government might properly take cognizance.

At this point it is pertinent to note that it is normal for a government or ruler, whether autocratic or democratic, to support those views (and the organized bodies of opinion holding them) which promise to gain the greatest volume of support. The history of the Byzantine empire in the three or four centuries after Constantine has numerous examples of attempts by the ruling institution to get doctrinal compromises accepted which would superficially unite opposing sectarian groups. This is a constant preoccupation of rulers, and it constantly fails after a short period of trial. Serious theological divergences spring from roots deep in a man's constitution, and, if a compromise does not satisfy the deep needs, men will sooner or later turn from it. Theological compromises are worked out intellectually from existing, partly contradictory, doctrinal formulations; but intellectual operations of this kind take account only of what is explicit in the formulations, whereas the formulations may be satisfactory only because of some elements which are not explicit but implicit. If the compromise formula does not make allowance for this implicit element, it will not satisfy those to whom at a deep level the implicit element was important. Frequently the compromise formula satisfies neither side.

These general considerations help one to understand a series of events which mark an important stage in the relations between the religious intellectuals and the government. The series of events is the Miḥna or Inquisition (833–849), during which government officials in certain important centres were required to make public profession of their adherence to the theological doctrine that the Qur'ān was created. The opposing doctrine was that the Qur'ān was the uncreated Speech of God. The government adopted this policy on the advice of a group of theologians of the Muʿtazilite sect who had become closely associated with it. Doubtless the government was attracted by the doctrine because it looked the kind of doctrine which would bring harmony between opposing political factions—between the constitutionalist bloc with the Islamic intellectuals on the one hand and the autocratic bloc with the secretaries on the other hand. The Muʿtazilites themselves were presumably looking for a way of reconciling the conflicting claims of reason and revelation—a genuine problem of the times with important practical consequences. But they did not go far enough to satisfy the deep inner demand of the Shīʿites for a charismatic leader, and at the same time their concession to the Shīʿites in depreciating the place of the Qur'ān alarmed those whose deep need was to belong to a charismatic community, since in denying that the Qur'ān was the eternal Speech of God they seemed to be denying that the community was divinely instituted.

In the course of the Inquisition most of the intellectuals who were required to make public profession of the doctrine did so, whatever their real views. A few refused, and of these some were put to death. The most important recusant was Aḥmad ibn-Ḥanbal (d. 855) who suffered in various ways but was not executed. Perhaps the authorities were aware of the great admiration for him among the populace of Baghdad. To later generations his successful passive resistance made him a hero, and it may be because of this, as much as because of his eminence as a jurist, that one of the four great Sunnite legal rites came to bear his name. Yet his example, though it showed that deeply-held conviction could not be changed by force, did not make his followers ready at all times to stand up for their convictions against government pressure. On the contrary, though they may occasionally have boldly maintained their convictions, the chief impression they give is that they were men anxious to gain government support. They also showed themselves quite unscrupulous in using the physical violence of mobs against their theological opponents.[12]

On the long-term view the chief result of the Inquisition was to make it clear that the government or ruling institution was stronger than the scholar-jurists. For some time before this it had been the instinct of the more sensitive members of this class or their predecessors to refuse all government appointments and all gifts from the caliphs; some were prepared to act as judges but without any financial emoluments. The wisdom of such an attitude was now apparent. So many of the scholar-jurists must now have been financially dependent on the ruling institution that they were unable as a body to resist pressure from it. Its abandonment of the policy of the Inquisition was therefore presumably not due to Aḥmad ibn-Ḥanbal and the Baghdad mob, but to the failure of the policy to win a sufficient volume of Shīʿite support. The change of policy meant the end of the political power of the Muʿtazilites and the beginning of their decline. When about 912 al-Ashʿarī left them and began to use their methods of argument to defend an essentially Ḥanbalite position, they ceased to be a significant factor in the theological life of the Islamic world, though they continued to exist for centuries. They may at times have suffered, along with certain philosophical coteries, from the disapproval of the government.[13]

A glimpse of the state of affairs about 922 is provided by Louis Massignon's study of the trial of al-Ḥallāj.[14] The political background of this trial was the political struggle for the position of vizier, which was mainly a struggle between two families, that of Ibn-al-Furāt (855–924) and ʿAlī ibn-ʿĪsā (859–945). Massignon describes the former as tending to an "absolutist" position and having moderate Shīʿite sympathies and the latter as being "constitutional" and broadly Sunnite; that is to say, they represented what were called above the "autocratic and constitutionalist blocs". It is further clear from Massignon's study that the qāḍīs or judges are mixed up in the politics of the time. Indeed the family of ʿAlī ibn-ʿĪsā is one of scholar-jurists or religious intellectuals which has made its way into the class of "secretaries" or administrators. His grandfather, Dā'ūd ibn-ʿAlī (d. 884), was the founder of the Ẓāhirite legal rite, while an uncle, Muḥammad ibn-Dā'ūd (d. 910), was vizier for a day in 908. Numerous details show that the religious intellectuals are now powerless against the vizier. It is their right to give legal opinions (*fatwās*), but the vizier can choose between conflicting opinions —and did so in respect of the condemnation of al-Ḥallāj. One scholar-jurist, Ibn-ʿAṭā, a follower of al-Ḥallāj, who made a public statement approving of the latter's creed, was roughly handled at the bidding of the vizier and beaten on the head with his own shoes until blood ran down his nostrils; whether as a consequence of this or not, he died a few days later.

Careful study of the condemnation of al-Ḥallāj seems to show that this was essentially a political decision. Muḥammad ibn-Dā'ūd was the author of a work which was composed round an anthology of poems, and of which the first half dealt with platonic love; this conception was absolutely opposed to the teaching of al-Ḥallāj about love for God.[15] When the case of al-Ḥallāj was judicially considered during the first vizierate of Ibn-al-Furāt (about 909), Muḥammad ibn-Dā'ūd, as head of the Ẓāhirite legal rite in succession to his father, gave a legal opinion (*fatwā*) condemning the doctrines of al-Ḥallāj. Behind this legal opinion, however, there was the hostility of Imāmite Shīʿite party and their leader, Abū-Sahl an-Nawbakhtī. In the course of his preaching al-Ḥallāj had tried to present his views to the Imāmites as a development of their own. Probably many of the rank and file were attracted to him. Perhaps Abū-Sahl, "with the scepticism and the discernment of an old politician", had for a time thought he might prove a useful instrument. Eventually, however, Abū-Sahl and the other Imāmite leaders became bitterly hostile to him. He acquired followers among the leading administrators, and gained a foothold at court, where the caliph had already shown Shīʿite sympathies. The Imāmites must have been seriously alarmed at the growth of this essentially Sunnite form of mysticism; its teaching that any man might rise to sanctity and obtain supernatural charismata cut the root from their doctrine that charismata were a special privilege of the ʿAlid line. The Imāmites, however, were unable to act directly against al-Ḥallāj, since no Imāmite jurist had any official authority and there was no subservient police force; and it is therefore remarkable that they were able to obtain Sunnite legal opinions condemning him.[16] The ultimate source of the condemnation of al-Ḥallāj is thus the political danger to the Imāmite party, the centre of the "autocratic bloc"; but what made it practicable was the political weakness of the Sunnite jurists and their readiness, where no clear principle was at stake, to please the ruling institution.

By 945 there had been an important change in the political situation. The caliph had lost most of his power and no longer appointed viziers who actually ruled. In Baghdad the supreme authority was in the hands of a family of Persian (Daylamite) war-lords, the Buwayhids (or Būyids), who had the title of "supreme commander" (*amīr al-umarāʾ*).[17] The Buwayhids were Shīʿites and represented the "autocratic bloc", but they were not able to make the territories they ruled completely Shīʿite, perhaps mainly because of the strong hold of Sunnism on the ordinary people. The Sunnite scholar-jurists retained most of their influence in the restricted field of law, but Shīʿite jurists were officially recognized along with them. Unfortunately this aspect of the Buwayhid period has not been fully studied, and it is impossible to go into further detail about it.[18]

While the Buwayhids still retained control of Baghdad a powerful state was being created in eastern Persia, Afghanistan and India by a war-lord of Turkish descent, Maḥmūd of Ghazna (*regnabat* 998–1030). One or two small incidents are recorded which may be taken as straws. At one point he summoned the Ashʿarite theologian Ibn-Fūrak (d. 1015) to Ghazna to reply to a charge of doctrinal error (in holding that Muḥammad's prophethood did not continue after his death).[19] On another occasion, after a drive against the Bāṭinites in Rayy, Maḥmūd appointed a reliable Sunnite scholar, Abū-Ḥātim ibn-Khāmūsh, as a kind of censor to examine the theological opinions of newcomers who wanted to settle in the town, before they were allowed to give public addresses.[20] This marks a turning of the tide again towards Sunnism, and the beginning of the support of Turkish rulers for it.

The resurgence of Sunnism in Baghdad and the lands dependent on it began about 1000 as Buwayhid power declined, and entered a new and decisive phase in 1055 when another dynasty of Turkish war-lords, the Seljūqs, gained control of Baghdad. At first, the influence of the Ḥanbalites was strongest, and under Tughril-Beg's vizier, al-Kundurī, curses against the Ash'arites were added to those against the Rāfiḍites (Imāmite Shī'-ites) in the Friday prayers.[21] The accession to the throne (the emirate) of Alp-Arslān in 1063 led to a change of policy. In his previous provincial governorship he had had as vizier the great Niẓām-al-Mulk, and the latter now became vizier of the whole empire and remained so, with increasing power, until his death in 1092. Niẓām-al-Mulk at once had the cursing of the Ash'arites stopped, and began to implement a policy of supporting and strengthening the Ash'arites against the other theological and legal schools. Towards the end of 1065 he began to build a college at Baghdad, which was opened in September 1067, and is known as the Niẓāmiyya. This is the college to which al-Ghazālī went as professor in 1091. Similar colleges were also founded in other important cities of the empire. Thus Ash'arite theology became the form of Islamic doctrine supported by the government.

Details have been preserved of the personal aspects of some of the theological disputes of the time, and these throw some light on the general conditions. In 1058 the wealthy and learned Traditionist al-Khaṭīb al-Baghdādī had to leave the city because of the difficulties made for him by the Ḥanbalites.[22] The opening of the Niẓāmiyya college in 1067 was the signal for fresh activity by the Ḥanbalites against both the Ashʿarites and the Muʿtazilites, whom they regarded as equally dangerous, since both practised *kalām* or rational theology. When in 1068 there was some question of the leading Muʿtazilite Abū-ʿAlī ibn-al-Walīd lecturing at the Niẓāmiyya, one of the Ḥanbalite leaders, the Sharīf Abū-Jaʿfar al-Hāshimī, organized a demonstration of protest which seems to have gained its end.[23] About the same time it came to light that one of the most promising young Ḥanbalites, Ibn-ʿAqīl, had been receiving instruction from Muʿtazilites, and a serious view was taken of this by some of the leaders, notably the same Abū-Jaʿfar al-Hāshimī. The matter aroused much public interest, and led to disturbances and minor riots, while Ibn-ʿAqīl had to lie low. The pressure on him was such that eventually in 1072 he made a retractation which satisfied the Sharīf Abū-Jaʿfar. There has recently been discovered and published the autograph diary of one of the lesser Ḥanbalites, with numerous entries covering about a year from 1068 to 1069; and this suggests that the Ḥanbalites were not so solidly against Ibn-ʿAqīl as had previously been thought, and that the pressure on him was not due to an official decision of the whole Ḥanbalite body but was mainly from the Sharīf Abū-Jaʿfar and his friends among the Ḥanbalites.[24]

Another series of incidents began with the visit to the Niẓāmiyya in 1067 of the Ashʿarite preacher, Abū-Naṣr al-Qushayrī (son of the well-known mystic Abū-'l-Qāsim al-Qushayrī). The Ḥanbalites stirred up riots in which twenty persons were killed. Once again the Sharīf Abū-Jaʿfar took a leading part in the attack, perhaps with some encouragement from his cousin, the caliph al-Muqtadī. The attacks were not confined to the preacher who was the original cause of the trouble, but included the senior professor at the Niẓāmiyya, Abū-Is'ḥāq ash-Shīrāzī. It is significant that the latter wrote to complain to Niẓām-al-Mulk himself and to obtain his backing. The vizier did his best to calm down the affair. He wrote pointing out how al-Ash'arī himself had shown great respect for Aḥmad ibn-Ḥanbal, and at the same time (perhaps at the request of the caliph) he summoned Abū-Naṣr al-Qushayrī back to Khurāsān—in any case the visit to Baghdad had been incidental to making the pilgrimage, but the scholars of the period were mobile, and he might have remained in Baghdad but for the storm.[25]

These details help to give some idea of conditions in Baghdad in the latter half of the eleventh century. Most prominent is the rivalry between the Ḥanbalites and the Ash'arites, which is in no way reduced by the official support given to both sides. It is also clear that an important section of the populace of Baghdad is behind the Ḥanbalites and is ready to stage a riot when given any encouragement. At the same time there are traces of serious differences within the Ḥanbalites. In general the policy of Niẓām-al-Mulk, as of all rulers, is to remove disharmonies as far as possible; but, though his backing of the Ash'arites was not unconditional, it doubtless added to the truculence of the Ḥanbalites. Apparently both parties concentrated their attention on maintaining and improving their position in Baghdad.

3 AL-GHAZĀLĪ'S CRITIQUE OF THE SCHOLAR-JURISTS

No one can read through, or even rapidly peruse, the opening book of al-Ghazālī's *Revival of the Religious*

Sciences without being struck by the bitterness of his criticisms of the scholar-jurists (including theologians) of his time. The first of the forty books of this lengthy work is entitled *Knowledge* (or *Science*), for which the Arabic is *'ilm*; and the corresponding agent-noun is *'ālim*, with the plural *'ulamā'* (often anglicized as "ulema"), which properly means "knower" or "scientist" but is here usually translated as "scholar-jurist". An understanding of these etymological connections helps one to realize the appropriateness of a critique of scholar-jurists in a book dealing with *Knowledge*.

This critique of the scholar-jurists is by no means a novel or original feature in the thought of al-Ghazālī. From the beginning the ascetic and mystical movement in Islam had made vigorous criticisms of the worldliness of the rulers of the Islamic empire and of those scholars who were prepared to take office (in such positions as judges) under the rulers. Under the Umayyad regime, while the class of religious intellectuals was still in embryo and they scarcely deserved to be called "scholar-jurists", a member of this group might act as judge temporarily on behalf of the caliph or a provincial governor, but he often did so without receiving any remuneration; this was presumably possible because he was still receiving a stipend from the state like all the other Muslims. The recognition given to the scholar-jurists at the beginning of the 'Abbāsid period (750 onwards), together with the apparent disappearance of the system of stipends, led to a new situation. The appointment of a scholar-jurist to a judgeship became a more frequent occurrence, but at the same time fewer of the scholar-jurists could afford to fulfil such duties without remuneration. A new Islamic educational system developed, directed to the study of the "religious sciences" and particularly of Islamic law; and those who were trained in this way normally expected a career in some branch of public service, or the administration of the empire. It was impossible, however, to be involved in the work of government without being infected by the worldliness, the love of wealth, power and honour, which was endemic in the ruling institution of a great empire.

Along with this more or less inevitable trend towards worldliness among those trained in the religious sciences there went a movement of protest. Some idea of its volume may be gained from the numerous quotations given by al-Ghazālī in the sixth chapter of the book mentioned.[26] These include sayings of the Companions of Muḥammad, such as the caliph ʻUmar. The earlier sayings, however, unless they are of a very general nature, are suspect as later inventions. A relatively early ascetic, al-Fuḍayl ibn-ʻIyāḍ (d. 803), is reported to have said that "wicked scholars will be dealt with first on the Resurrection Day, even before the idol-worshippers": and this may well be genuine. From other sources we learn how he boldly criticized and upbraided Hārūn ar-Rashīd to his face; and a remark of his about avoiding Qur'ān-reciters since their evidence would be accepted against one seems to imply his awareness of the consequences of a measure of public recognition of this minor section of the religious institution.[27] Somewhat later Yaḥyā ibn-Muʻādh ar-Rāzī (d. 871) complained that "the glory of science and wisdom departs when they are used to gain this world", and taunted the "men of science" with "having castles like Caesar's, mansions like Chosroes', . . . doctrines like Satan's, and no place for Muḥammad's law".[28] Another bold ascetic, Ḥātim the Deaf (d. 851), publicly shamed the judge of Rayy (Rey, in Persia) in his own audience-chamber because of the ostentatious luxury in which he lived.[29] Criticisms of worldly and hypocritical scholars are to be found in the extant works of men like al-Ḥārith ibn-Asad al-

Muḥāsibī (d. 857) and Abū-Ṭālib al-Makkī (d. 996).[30]

In view of all this it might be thought that al-Ghazālī was merely repeating customary criticisms. The vehemence of his expressions, however, leads one to think that this was something about which he had strong personal feelings; and this impression is confirmed by the fact that he devotes most of the preface of *The Revival of the Religious Sciences* to commenting on the shortcomings of contemporary "scientists", that is, the scholar-jurists. He addresses this preface to one who is inclined to blame those like himself who for reasons of piety turn from worldliness and from the worldly scholars (of the religious sciences) who, according to Tradition, would be the persons most severely punished on Resurrection Day. Then he continues:

"Indeed, there is no cause for your persistence in pride apart from the disease, common to the multitudes of ordinary men, of failing to notice the essence of this matter and not realizing how important and serious it is. The world-to-come is advancing and this-world receding; the time (of death) is near, the journey long, the provisions deficient, the danger great and the road blocked. Everything save knowledge and action sincerely for the sake of God by a clear-sighted critic (of himself) is rejected. To travel the road of the world-to-come without guide or companion, when its mischances are so many, is wearisome and laborious. The guides for the way are the ulema, who are the heirs of the prophets. But this age is bereft of them; there remain only those who are such in outward seeming; over most of them Satan has gained mastery. Their rebellious nature has deceived them. Each has become greatly desirious of his present transient lot. He has come to consider good evil and evil good, so that religious knowledge has been obliterated and the light of guidance in various parts of the world quenched. They have led men to suppose that there is no knowledge (or science) except a *legal-opinion* (*fatwā*) of the government by which the judges are helped to settle a quarrel of the plebeian masses; or else *argument*, by which the seeker of glory is armed for knock-out victory; or else meretricious *saj'* (ornate rhymed prose), by which the preacher deceives the ordinary people. Apart from these three things there is no snare to hunt forbidden (pleasures) and no net to catch worldly vanities.

"The science of the road of the world-to-come, on the other hand, and the learning, wisdom, knowledge, illumination, light, guidance and direction, as God calls them in scripture, by which the noble Muslims of old lived their lives, have become rejected among men and completely forgotten. Since this is a grave weakness in a religion and a black mark against it, I thought it right to busy myself with composing this book, out of a concern for the revival of the religious sciences, to show the practices of the former leaders, and to make clear the limits of the useful sciences in the eyes of the prophets and the noble Muslims of old."[31]

Throughout the book of *Knowledge* al-Ghazālī never allows the readers to forget his critical attitude towards the scholar-jurists of the day. His discussion of the various branches of religious knowledge (in chapter 2) culminates in an assessment of them by the criterion of how far they help to fit a man for the life of the world-to-come. The same conception becomes a basis (in the following chapter) for deciding how far it is good to pursue any particular branch; while the long sixth chapter points the contrast between the ulema of this-world and the ulema of the world-to-come. The following are the chief points made by al-Ghazālī.

(1) Most of the religious knowledge of the day, as

studied by the scholar-jurists, is purely this-worldly and deals only with such matters as the ordering of the life of society. From what al-Ghazālī says, it appears that they were in the habit of spending much time and energy in the discussion of legal points which had little practical application; for example, details for formulae of divorce which were perhaps rarely used, or questions concerning fine points of "difference" between the recognized legal rites. (It should be noted, however, that in respect of such matters our general knowledge of the period is scanty and does not enable us to do more than make deductions from al-Ghazālī's own words.) While those who claim to be religious scholars thus exercise themselves in academic trifles, they neglect the real business of religion, the preparation of man for the life of the world-to-come. Those who are so learned about rare forms of divorce can tell you nothing about the simpler things of the spiritual life, such as the meaning of sincerity towards God or trust in him (*ikhlās*, *tawakkul*).

(2) The attempt of such men to justify their conduct on religious grounds is unsatisfactory. They say that this is a "communal obligation" (*farḍ kifāya*), that is, something which ought to be done by some unspecified members of the community for the sake of the whole, but which is not incumbent on every one as is an "individual obligation" (*farḍ ʿayn*). But al-Ghazālī points out that it is not for a Muslim to undertake a "communal obligation" until he has performed all his "individual obligations", and that too many persons are performing this "communal obligation" while certain other "communal obligations", such as being a doctor in a small town, are neglected—there are many towns where the only doctors are Jews and Christians, persons not qualified to give evidence in a Muslim law-court. So al-Ghazālī concludes that it is not zeal for the performance

of "communal obligations" that leads so many to become scholar-jurists.

(3) The corollary of this is that in fact the majority of the religious scholars of the day are chiefly concerned with their professional qualifications as a means of gaining wealth, power and position. This is really the heart of his critique. The intellectuals of the age have become infected by the worldliness of the rulers. This is a worse fault, however, in those who claim to be religious scholars, for it means that they are hypocritical and do not practise what they preach. Among al-Ghazālī's quotations is one from a poet not named which echoes the Gospel saying about the salt which has lost its savour: "O reciters (of the Qur'ān), O salt of the city, what use is salt, if the salt is corrupted?"[32]

(4) Al-Ghazālī further holds that the true scholar will have nothing to do with rulers and will not accept offices from them. The true scholar will even avoid having to give a formal legal-opinion when he is asked to do so—presumably because this was part of the official legal procedure and indeed of the business of government.[33] He even held that the religious scholar should teach freely without any remuneration.[34]

(5) While al-Ghazālī has this generally critical attitude, he does not entirely condemn the study of the various branches of religious knowledge. They have their uses, even if these are restricted to the ordering of society in this world. What is important is not to forget that man's true destiny is in the world-to-come, and, in the light of this, to allow the usefulness of each branch of religious knowledge to determine the extent to which it is studied.

A further criticism of the religious intellectuals of the time is implicit in another work by al-Ghazālī, *The Decisive Criterion for distinguishing between Islam and Unbelief*, which was composed some time after *The Revival of the Religious Sciences.* It was apparently the custom for various schools of thought among the theologians to regard as an unbeliever anyone who disagreed with them on some comparatively minor point. Al-Ghazālī complains that men are being too light-hearted in calling other Muslims unbelievers, since this is an assertion with serious legal consequences—it is not a crime to kill an unbeliever. Part of the trouble is that, if one defines "unbelief" as "regarding Muḥammad as false in any part of his message", then each party can show how the others regard as false some parts of what it considers to be the message. This leads to a discussion of "interpretation" and five different senses of "existence". From this standpoint the disputes between sects such as those mentioned are seen to be about canons of interpretation. Al-Ghazālī proposes the eirenic solution that, so long as a man accepts the basic credal statements *in some sense* he cannot be called an "unbeliever", but at most "erring" or "heretical".

It has also to be noticed that, especially during the period of his professorship at Baghdad from July 1091 to November 1095, al-Ghazālī was deeply involved both in the worldliness of the intellectuals and in the dependence on the government which he later criticized. The teacher to whom he owed most, al-Juwaynī, had himself been appointed by the vizier, Niẓām-al-Mulk, to the latter's new college at Nishapur, as part of his policy of encouraging and supporting Ash'arite theologians. On al-Juwaynī's death in July 1085 al-Ghazālī had gone to the "camp" of the vizier, and had apparently spent the following six years in his entourage. It was Niẓām-al-Mulk who was responsible for his appointment to the professorship in Baghdad. In Baghdad he was at the official ceremony of taking the oath to the new caliph, al-Mustaẓ'hir, in February 1094, and was sufficiently well known to him to be asked by him to write a polemical work against the Bāṭinites. Thus al-Ghazālī had known something of the favour of rulers. It may also be that after the deaths of Niẓām-al-Mulk and the sultan Malikshāh in the autumn of 1092 he found relations with the rulers difficult. There was fighting between members of the Seljūq family, and it was not till about February 1095 that Barkiyāruq was finally recognized in Baghdad. The caliph and al-Ghazālī had shown some support for other candidates for supreme power, and al-Ghazālī would therefore be suspect to the government after February 1095.

During this period he must also have known something of the fierce rivalries between the scholar-jurists of Baghdad, especially between the Ḥanbalites and the Ashʿarites. The Ḥanbalites seem to have been still furious at the very existence of the Niẓāmiyya college and at everyone connected with it. Even between the professors there personal difficulties seem to have been considerable. One of the men whom al-Ghazālī seems to have replaced had been appointed only the year before, but was brought back after al-Ghazālī's departure. Politics doubtless entered into the appointment and demotion of professors in ways which have not been properly studied, and for the study of which adequate materials may not be available.

For men in such circumstances their whole careers would depend on worldly calculations of political advantage and disadvantage. It would be difficult for them to be immersed in such a life and not to accept in full the values of this section of society. Thus personal experience of this kind of life is a large part of the ground for al-Ghazālī's criticism of the scholar-jurists. Similarly, his advice to have nothing to do with rulers must be the outcome of some deep disillusionment with governmental support.

4 DOGMATIC THEOLOGY FROM A NEW STANDPOINT

(a) *General Attitude to Theology*

After the study of the Qur'ān, at first mainly by memorizing, the staple of higher education—education in the "Islamic sciences"—was jurisprudence with its subordinate disciplines, such as the study of Traditions and traditionists. Theology or *kalām* was like a "special subject", somewhat beyond the usual curriculum, to which only a few outstanding students would give prolonged attention. Of all the men named as being teachers of al-Ghazālī only al-Juwaynī seems to have lectured to him in theology. This must have been in the years immediately preceding the death of al-Juwaynī in 1085. It is unlikely that after this al-Ghazālī met anyone who influenced his theological development, except negatively by stating views which he felt bound to criticize.

Chronologically these well-attested facts fit in with the account al-Ghazālī gives in *Deliverance from Error*, except for the fact that he speaks of having written some books about theology, whereas his extant theological works, notably one which may be called *The Golden Mean in Belief*, are clearly subsequent to his study of philosophy (as will presently be explained in detail). It is possible that, when he wrote this, al-Ghazālī was thinking about books on the principles of jurisprudence. On other grounds, however, it seems certain that *Deliverance from Error* is arranged schematically and does not follow the strict chronological order. When this is admitted, there is no further difficulty about the relation of the autobiographical statements to the extant works. There is an important consequence, however, namely that we have no information about al-Ghazālī's theological views until after he had studied philosophy and was well on the way to becoming a ṣūfī. The major extant work is the book just mentioned, *The Golden Mean in Belief*, and it cannot have been written earlier than the summer of 1095, just before he left Baghdad. It quotes *The Inconsistency of the Philosophers* (completed in January 1095) and other books of about the same time; its use of syllogisms shows that it is subsequent to his study of Aristotelian logic; and the impression of a careful scholar like Maurice Bouyges was that the writer's preoccupations were the same as in the *Inconsistency*.[35] On the other hand, *The Golden Mean* is prior to the *Revival*, since it is mentioned there.

Now we know something about al-Ghazālī's later attitude to theology from what he says about it in *Deliverance from Error*.[36] There he makes two main points. Firstly, the aim of the theologians was to defend dogma against heretical aberrations and innovations. Secondly, the theologians failed to meet the logical demands of those who had studied Aristotelian logic, since their arguments were directed against those who already shared their own point of view to a considerable extent. He had already spoken of this limited aim of theology in the *Revival*, while also emphasizing that theology contributed nothing to the actual practice of the religious life.[37] That he felt something of this inadequacy of theology as he wrote *The Golden Mean* is suggested by the prayer at the end: "We pray God that he will not make this of ill outcome for us, but will place it in the balance of good deeds when our acts are given back to us".[38] Nevertheless the references to it in the *Revival* and other later works show that he continued to regard it as valuable so far as it went. In a short summary of the *Revival* he has an interesting description of it. He is speaking of three possible attitudes towards the doctrines of the creed: firstly, belief or simple acceptance, then knowledge of their proofs and finally knowledge of their mysteries. After mentioning the statement of the creed in the *Revival*, he goes on: "as for the proofs . . . we have set them down in *The Golden Mean in Belief* in some hundred pages; it is a book devoted entirely to this main matter (?), containing the essence of the science of the theologians, but more adequate in its proofs and more apt to knock at the doors of knowledge (of the mysteries) than the official (or normal) theology which is met in the books of the theologians".[39]

The conclusion to which these reflections lead is that the statements in *Deliverance from Error* about rejecting theology and turning from it have to be understood in a restricted sense. Al-Ghazālī was dissatisfied with theology because it contributed little or nothing to the attainment of that goal of the individual life which he described as "salvation" or the bliss of Paradise. But he thought that it had a prophylactic function in the life of the community, and, in so far as this was so, he continued to hold the views of the Ash'arite school to which he had always belonged. There is no evidence in the works generally accepted as authentic that in his closing years he abandoned Ash'arite doctrines for the Neoplatonism he had refuted in *The Inconsistency of the Philosophers*. On the contrary, the date which has been found for a small work called *The Restraining of the Commonalty from the Science of Theology* sets the completion of this work only a few days before his death. There seem to be no strong grounds for not accepting this date. The book implies that the theology which ordinary men are to be kept away from is Sunnite theology, and might be looked on as an elaboration of a point of view already expressed in *The Golden Mean*.[40] In other words, although al-Ghazālī thought the importance of theology had been greatly exaggerated, he continued to take up a theological position which was broadly Ash'arite.

(b) *Al-Ghazālī's Exposition of His Theological Views*

In studying al-Ghazālī's dogmatic theology the chief interest is in noticing the contrast between his exposition and that of al-Juwaynī. For this purpose we have, by al-Juwaynī, *The Right Guidance*,[41] a work of about twice the length of al-Ghazālī's *Golden Mean* and covering much the same ground—both works are of what has been called the Summa Theologica type. In addition we have *The Niẓāmian Creed*,[42] which covers most of the subjects of *The Golden Mean* in about half the compass. According to the manuscript, however, this book is the version of a young Spanish scholar who had it from al-Ghazālī in Baghdad, presumably between 1093 and 1095. This would mean that this was the book which al-Ghazālī used as a text for his lectures; in the main it must be al-Juwaynī's book, but al-Ghazālī may have made slight modifications here and there.[43] Proceeding on the assumption that it is essentially the work of al-Juwaynī, we note that it stands somewhere between *The Right Guidance* and *The Golden Mean*; the author has become interested in some of the problems raised by the philosophers, but he does not deal with philosophical objections nearly so fully as al-Ghazālī. This confirms the reports that al-Juwaynī introduced al-Ghazālī to the study of philosophy.[44]

In his own exposition al-Ghazālī follows the standard plan for the arrangement of topics in such treatises.[45] He has four parts or chapters dealing respectively with the proof of the existence of a Creator, the attributes of God, the relations of God and man, and questions connected with prophethood and the imamate (or leadership of the Islamic community). In addition he has four prefaces, in the fourth of which he briefly explains the nature of syllogism.

The early pages dealing with the proof of the existence of God are sufficient to show how completely al-Ghazālī had accepted the syllogism as the primary form of argument. Thus his essential proof of the existence of God is:

> "Every originated thing has a cause.
> The world is an originated thing.
> Therefore the world has a cause."

He then considers how we know the two premisses. The major premiss he regards as a necessary first principle. The minor premiss he proves by another syllogism:

> "Everything not-without-originated-things is originated.
> Every body is not-without-originated-things.
> Therefore every body is originated."

He then points out that the dispute with the philosophers is over the major premiss here, and proceeds to discuss it further. All this is in sharp contrast with al-Juwaynī's basic argument: an originated-thing may exist or not exist; therefore it requires a determinant, to determine whether it is to exist or not exist at a particular time. This determinant may be either a cause (*'illa*), or a nature (*ṭabī'a*) or a conscious agent; various arguments show that it is not a cause or a nature; therefore it must be a conscious agent. This method of enumerating possibilities exhaustively and then eliminating all but one was very popular with al-Ghazālī's predecessors, and al-Juwaynī was still attached to it. On a minor point he has what is tantamount to a syllogism:

> "What does not precede originated-things is originated.
> Substances do not precede accidents (which are originated).

Therefore the world (the totality of substances and accidents) is originated."

Al-Juwaynī, however, does not call attention to the special form of this argument. If, as is possible, he had some elementary knowledge of syllogistic logic, he did not realize its superiority to the methods of argument traditional among Islamic theologians.[46]

The importance of the syllogism was not so much in respect of particular arguments as of the system as a whole. There is a certain order in syllogistic reasoning. The premiss of one syllogism may be the conclusion of another, and this other is then logically prior. If the order of priority is not duly observed, there is a vicious circle in the reasoning. While there could be chains of reasoning according to the older logic, there was not the same over-all order. Each chain of argument tends to be treated as an isolated unit, and propositions are asserted without considering whether they are logically prior or posterior to others. Al-Juwaynī has a section proving that God is not a body, directed mainly against Muslim anthropomorphists; and he then follows it with one on substance directed mainly against the Christians. Al-Ghazālī changes this order; he first proves that God is not a substance (or atom), and then neatly adds that he cannot be a body, since a body is two or more substances.[47] In particular, attention may be directed to a remark by al-Juwaynī that "if you call God a body, you either contradict the proof of the originatedness of substances, since this proof is based on their being receptive of composition, contiguity and separation, or . . ." In a syllogistic system the point could have been made more vigorously, since there could have been a reference to a proposition already proved; here, because of the lack of a recognized order, there is some suggestion of uncertainty about previous conclusions. When in

Deliverance from Error al-Ghazālī notes that the philosophers do not manage to prove all their metaphysical views syllogistically, this is an indication of his intense interest in logic and of the attention he paid to the logical aspects of others' thought and his own. This concern for logical method and logical order leads to many changes in the detail of his proofs, compared with those of al-Juwaynī.

The other point to be commented on is al-Ghazālī's much greater awareness of the philosophers as opponents, and a corresponding reduction of emphasis on arguments against other adversaries. In *The Right Guidance* al-Juwaynī makes practically no attempt to argue against the Neoplatonic philosophers. In *The Niẓāmian Creed* the philosophical conceptions of the necessary, the possible and the impossible are in the forefront, and a measure of attention is given to the positions of the philosophers. But al-Ghazālī's study of philosophy had brought into his ken a whole new world of objections, and this is apparent in his exposition of theology, especially in the proofs of the existence of God.[48]

These two points—the conscious basing of the arguments on syllogistic logic, and the attention to objections from a Neoplatonic standpoint—are in fact al-Ghazālī's great contributions to the later development of Islamic theology. From now onwards all the rational theologians in Islam wrote in a way which assumed a philosophical outlook in pre-theological matters, and often explicitly discussed such matters. Indeed in some of the treatises the philosophical preliminaries occupy by far the larger part of the work, so that the impression is given that the authors were more interested in the philosophy than in the actual theology.

From another point of view it might be asserted that what al-Ghazālī had done was to effect a complete fusion of the Greek and Islamic intellectual traditions. This refers, of course, to the Greek tradition in the form in which it was still alive in the lands of the ʿAbbāsid caliphate. While there is much truth in the assertion, it must not be allowed to make us think that the philosophers were essentially an alien element in the population and that al-Ghazālī made their disciplines available for "native" thinkers. There was much that was common to the philosophers and the theologians. Both believed in rational argument. The difference was that the philosophers had elaborated logic more fully and were more conscious of what they were doing. The theologians, however, had also given some thought to logic, though perhaps more in the sphere of jurisprudence than of theology proper (but all theologians were also competent in jurisprudence). Thus it would be wrong to say that "more up-to-date" or "more scientific" methods were incorporated into theology, for thus we should be importing our own values. Both sides had the same values, but the philosophers had realized them more fully.

The real opposition, at least in Baghdad, was the Ḥanbalite school of theology, which was still suspicious of rational argument in any form, and continued to be so. The most remarkable expression of this line of thought is in *The Refutation of the Logicians* by Ibn-Taymiyya (d. 1328). What is remarkable is that, though the author finds weaknesses in Aristotelian logic with great skill and acumen, he does not use his obvious mastery of the subject to provide a superior logic, but to urge the abandonment altogether of the attempt to systematize the material of revelation (in the Qur'ān and the Traditions) and to defend it rationally. This distrust of reason is an important trend to be found in Western civilization as well as in Islam. It is still alive in Islam in the Wahhābites of Arabia and other fundamentalists. In the West the protest against excessive rationalism has been taken up by existentialism, and this is perhaps the nearest man can come to the statement of a rational case for distrusting reason.

The new perspective introduced by al-Ghazālī into Islamic theology, then, became part of its permanent nature. In this we see one important aspect of the growth of a theology. The theologian at any given time is producing replies to the objections raised by the opponents of his religion. These opponents attack him at every possible point. Some of their criticisms will be stronger than others; some of his replies will be more effective than others. All this he hands on to his successor, who is usually his pupil. Where the replies have been effective, the pupil repeats them; if he can think of better ones he substitutes them; and he has also to add new replies to new criticisms. Thus the theology of a religious community is constantly growing. It retains all that is satisfactory in the work of past theologians. There may be less emphasis on old arguments, since the bearers of the criticisms to which they were replies may have died out—but there is always the chance that someone may revive an old objection, or that it may crop up in a new form. So in its intellectual basis a religious community retains something of all its past—of its responses to the varying situations through which it defined itself. There is even a sense in which the continued existence of different intellectual traditions within a community (such as fundamentalist and rational-theological) is part of its definition of itself. From this standpoint we begin to realize the vastness of al-Ghazālī's contribution to present-day Islam.

VI

THE BITTERNESS OF WORLDLY SUCCESS

INTRODUCTORY NOTE

In the course of the year 1095 al-Ghazālī had what would now be called a "breakdown". Although it was essentially a psychological or spiritual crisis, it came to a head in July of that year when physical symptoms—an inability to utter words—forced him to abandon lecturing. Since some of his books must be ascribed to about this date, it is probable that he was able to continue writing. After much hesitation he at length came to a decision. In November 1095 he set out from Baghdad and made for Syria, thereby abandoning his professorship and his position as a public figure in order to lead what was in effect a monastic life.[1] In order to understand this astonishing step, we must look at the previous history of the ṣūfī or mystical-monastic movement.[2]

VI

THE BITTERNESS OF WORLDLY SUCCESS

I THE ṢŪFĪ MOVEMENT

THE word *ṣūfī* is an adjective from *ṣūf*, wool, and its common meaning is derived from the fact that from the ninth century the practice of wearing a white woollen robe became normal among Muslim mystics. Both the practice and the word are found in the eighth century, but they were then exceptional.[3] There is an important sense, of course, in which Islamic mysticism begins with Muḥammad himself. It is difficult to be certain about details, for all we have to go on is what we deduce from the Qur'ān and from the Traditions—and the Traditions themselves are often dubious. Yet in general it is clear that Muḥammad had profound mystical experiences, which both stirred him to the depths and were a source of spiritual power to him. How his experiences are to be described in terms of the later systematization of "stations" and "states" is a question that may be neglected here; for one thing he was probably much less conscious of his inner life than were the later mystics. What is beyond doubt is that his inner experiences were such that they gave him a firm conviction that God was real. This conviction supported the basic Islamic conception of the true nature of human life—activity in accordance with God's commands, leading to the eternal bliss of Paradise.[4]

From the lifetime of Muḥammad onwards, there were Muslims to whom the element of piety or spirituality in the Qur'ān made a strong appeal. In the earliest days such Muslims were nearly all Arabs. With the conversion of the inhabitants of Iraq there came into Islam many persons who had been in touch with the Christian mystical tradition; and it is mainly among non-Arabs that mysticism in the strict sense develops. The most prominent figure of the seventh and early eighth century was al-Ḥasan al-Baṣrī (643–728).[5] While most of his thought and teaching is along the line of asceticism, he occasionally touches on the conception of love towards God. He had a great influence on his contemporaries and successors, and the names and sayings have been recorded of many ascetic-mystics who lived during the eighth and ninth centuries.

Other important figures are those of al-Junayd (d. 910) and al-Ḥallāj (d. 922). Although the latter was executed for heresy, Louis Massignon, who has studied his life and teaching in great detail, maintains that his essential aim (and also that of al-Junayd) was to make the spiritual energy generated in the lives of the ascetics and mystics a fructifying and vitalizing agency in the life of the whole community as it pursued its essential aim of living according to God's commands and thereby attaining Paradise.[6] The position of these two men is in contrast to various aberrations which Massignon labels intellectualism, libertarianism, dualism and monism.[7] These faults may occur in combination. Intellectualism is exaggeration of the importance of the human intellect or reasoning faculty (at the expense of revelation). Similarly libertarianism is exaggeration of the importance of the human will and human effort. It is often associated with monism, that is, exaggeration of God's immanence, leading to assertions of the mystic's identity with God. A notable example of this is the celebrated or notorious Abū-Yazīd al-Bisṭāmī (d. 875), who gives the impression of aiming at control of the world of inner experience through his own efforts, employing various ascetical practices and techniques (some perhaps derived from India).[8] The fourth aberration, dualism, is undue exaggeration of God's transcendence and is found in circles usually regarded as theologically conservative.

There was much mysticism during the tenth and eleventh centuries. Mysticism had become a part of the general life of the Islamic community. It was not something separated and isolated, as some Western accounts of the subject suggest, but belonged to the ordinary life of Muslims. Occasionally little coteries of ṣūfīs might withdraw into seclusion; but at the same time a surprisingly large number of the scholar-jurists, of whom there are biographical notices, are said to have been ṣūfīs. In other words, the mystics were not a sect apart but shared in the disputes of the community about matters of theology and jurisprudence and included men of the most divergent views in these respects. Thus the struggle between the various mystical doctrines or "aberrations" was not entirely cut off from the other intellectual struggles of the period. The most outstanding mystic of the century before al-Ghazālī is probably al-Qushayrī (d. 1072), who was also a Shāfiʿite jurist. Like several other men, he aimed at a synthesis of Ashʿarite dogmatics and certain mystical elements, but his synthesis is adjudged "insufficient" by Massignon.[9] The situation demanded a radical rethinking of the whole of Islamic theology, and the conservative ethos of Islam made this incredibly difficult. Al-Ghazālī later made a more strenuous effort of the same kind, but whether he was more successful must remain doubtful.

One of the aspects of the ṣūfī movement to which comparatively little attention has been given is its relation to contemporary history and social conditions. It is held that the early ascetic trends were a reaction to the wealth and luxury which came to the leading men of the Islamic empire along with their vast conquests;[10] and this seems to be true of the earliest period. A little later there are traces of attacks by the ascetics and mystics on the worldliness and hypocrisy of the scholar-jurists.[11] In a way the faults of these men were more serious than those of a ruler, for they were the heart and conscience of Islamic society. From the first, Islam had been protesting against worldliness and the materialistic pursuit of wealth (in the case of the rich merchants of Mecca), and it was thus a disaster for its spiritual leaders to become worldly and materialistic.

It is permissible to wonder why, about the year 900, there should have been a flowering of the higher mysticism in men like al-Junayd and al-Ḥallāj; but the most that can be done here is to give some simple suggestions towards a solution of the problem. It seems most likely that here, as in the general study of the life of al-Ghazālī, fuller understanding is to be gained by attending closely to the position of the scholar-jurists in the community and their attitudes to the rulers and the common people. Much had been happening in the ninth century. At the beginning there had been the work of ash-Shāfiʿī in bringing greater objectivity to the bases of law by insisting on Traditions, duly transmitted, of the words or acts of Muḥammad. This produced later in the century the standard collections of "sound Traditions" by al-Bukhārī (d. 870) and Muslim (d. 875). By giving greater intellectual coherence to legal doctrine these developments must have strengthened the position of the scholar-jurists, but at the same time must have made them more of a closed corporation. The latter point has its sinister aspect when it is remembered that the Miḥna or Inquisition of 833–849 had demonstrated the complete domination of the scholar-jurists as a class and corporation by the rulers. The Inquisition was eventually given up for reasons of state and not because of the resistance of Aḥmad ibn-Ḥanbal and one or two others.

From this time on the scholar-jurists, with hardly any exceptions, are wholly subservient to the government. Men who have not the courage to stand for Islamic law in its purity soon lose their zeal for that purity; instead, they become filled with desires for worldly wealth, position and power.[12]

The years from about 900 to 1100 saw fresh vicissitudes. For half a century or more after 945 Baghdad was under the rule of the Shīʿite Buwayhid sultans. Though the Sunnite scholar-jurists continued to have official recognition, their power was somewhat less, and it was difficult to maintain even this without becoming more involved in court intrigues. All this would tend to make the scholar-jurists still more self-seeking. After the unsettled years that followed the decline in Buwayhid power, the advent of the Seljūqs in 1055 brought a measure of peace. When a little later the Seljūq government, guided by Niẓām-al-Mulk, decided to support and indeed promote Ashʿarism, the dependence of the scholar-jurists on the rulers was, if anything, increased. The merging of the class of scholar-jurists with that of secretaries (civil servants), which had been proceeding for at least two centuries, was almost completed. One of the results was the succumbing of the scholar-jurists to the politicians' disease of worldliness and materialism —an epidemic to which al-Ghazālī's criticisms[13] bear witness.

This then is the situation in which the ṣūfī movement flourished. The ṣūfīs were those members of the intellectual class who had a genuine spiritual concern which had not been choked and killed by worldliness. The forces of worldliness were so strong in political and judicial circles that it was impossible for such men to express their spiritual aspirations in public activity. Moreover in many respects a superficial conformity with minimum Islamic standards had been attained.

In these circumstances it was natural that the higher spiritual aspirations should seek to express themselves in the cultivation of the inner life. Here they were free from the domination of the "system"—the rigidified body of Islamic legal thought—with all the worldly and materialistic political attitudes now associated with it. In certain cases such a turning from public activity to the inner life would rightly be regarded as escapism—a refusal to face up to difficulties. Here, however, the change seems to be justified. On the one hand, the worldliness woven into the context of social and political life made it virtually impossible to realize further spiritual aims in an external way in this context. On the other hand, the vision of man and his place in the universe (which was the essence of Islam) had guided and inspired men to a realization of the vision in the external forms of Islamic society, and this very success suggested the need for a switch to greater emphasis on the inner life and the channelling of efforts in this direction. Thus the adoption of the mystic life is not simply a refusal to face difficulties. The spiritual vision which had hitherto guided the development of Islamic religion was itself pointing to greater concentration on the inner life.

2 THE CRISIS OF 1095

In his autobiography, *Deliverance from Error*, al-Ghazālī appears to say that he turned to the study of ṣūfism only after he had found no satisfaction in his study of theology, philosophy and Bāṭinism. Despite this, however, he must have had contacts with ṣūfism at a much earlier period. The guardian to whom he and his brother were entrusted on his father's death is called a ṣūfī.[14] While he was a student at Ṭūs, also, he seems to have had as a spiritual director a man called Yūsuf an-Nassāj, to whom he related his dreams and by whom his character was "polished"; unfortunately nothing more is known about this man.[15] Al-Juwaynī, under whom al-Ghazālī was studying theology at Nishapur from 1077 to 1085, was sympathetic to ṣūfism. Another professor at Nishapur at this period, under whom al-Ghazālī worked, was al-Fārmadhī; though some of his lectures may have been on jurisprudence (which he had studied under the elder al-Ghazālī), he was a pupil of al-Qushayrī and had become a recognized leader of the ṣūfīs in Ṭūs and Nishapur.[16] He had been accepted by Niẓām-al-Mulk, and indeed his standing with him was such that he was able to criticize the vizier's faults to his face.[17] Since another of his pupils was the son (al-Ḥasan) of al-Ghazālī's first teacher of jurisprudence at Ṭūs (Aḥmad ar-Rādhakānī),[18] it is clear that al-Ghazālī was moving in circles that were very favourable to ṣūfism. It is also clear, however, that after some instruction and a limited amount of mystical practice al-Ghazālī became more interested in theology and philosophy and neglected mysticism.[19]

According to *Deliverance from Error* al-Ghazālī was greatly concerned in his student days and in the immediately following years with the quest for certainty. His first crisis, when for a time he was a complete sceptic, arose from the realization that the methods he had been employing did not give absolute certainty. He had probably begun the study of philosophy before this crisis, and he may have reached the point of seeing that in theology and metaphysics the philosophers did not follow a strict logical method. At the close of the period of scepticism he found himself able to accept some basic principles because of a "light from God"; as we might put it, he saw directly, or had an immediate intuition, that these principles were true. In 1095 when the second crisis came upon him he already had a steadfast faith in God, prophethood and the Last Day.[20] Despite his way of putting things in *Deliverance from Error*, which makes it appear that he was making a personal search for truth in his study of Bāṭinism, it seems unlikely that there was much personal engagement; he was primarily fulfilling a duty imposed on him by the caliph, though in doing so he may have come to understand more fully the place of Muḥammad in the community. In keeping with all this the crisis of 1095 came upon him at a time when his dominant aim was not to find intellectual certainty but to achieve a satisfying life, a life worthy of Paradise. This may be seen from his own description of the crisis, of which the following is an abbreviated version.[21]

"Lastly I turned to the way of the mystics. I knew that in their path there has to be both knowledge and activity, and that the object of the latter is to purify the self from vices and faults of character. Knowledge was easier for me than activity. I began by reading their books . . . and obtained a thorough intellectual understanding of their principles. Then I realized that what is most distinctive of them can be attained only by personal experience ('taste'—*dhawq*), ecstasy and a change of character. . . . I saw clearly that the mystics were men of personal experience not of words, and that I had gone as far as possible by way of study and intellectual application, so that only personal experience and walking in the mystic way were left.

"In my previous studies and in my practical living I had reached a steadfast faith in God, prophethood and the Last Day; and these principles had become firmly fixed in me not through logical proof but by various external and internal causes which cannot be comprehended in detail. I was convinced that the happiness of the world to come is to be attained only by a God-fearing life and the discipline of desire, and that the essential thing is to sever the attachment of the heart to this world by turning from the sphere of deception to that of eternity, and by earnestly seeking to draw near to God. This could only be done, too, by rejecting wealth and position and by escaping from entanglements and commitments.

"When I considered my circumstances, I saw I was deeply involved in affairs, and that the best of my activities, my teaching, was concerned with branches of knowledge which were unimportant and worthless. I also examined my motive in teaching and saw that it was not sincere desire to serve God but that I wanted an influential position and widespread recognition. I was in no doubt that I stood on an eroding sandbank, and was in imminent danger of hell-fire if I did not busy myself with mending my ways.

"I kept thinking about this for a time, as long as it remained a matter of choice. One day I would decide to leave Baghdad and escape from my involvements; the next day I would give up the decision. I would put one foot forward, and draw the other back. Whenever morning found me with a genuine longing to seek the world to come, evening saw it reduced to nothing by the attack of a host of desires. Worldly desires were trying to keep me chained where I was, while the herald of faith was summoning, 'To the road! To the road! Little of life is left, and before you is a long journey. Your intellectual and practical involvements are hypocrisy and delusion. If you do not prepare for the future life now, when will you prepare; if you do not sever your attachments now, when will you sever them?' At this I would be roused to make a firm decision to run away and escape. Afterwards Satan would return and say, 'This is a passing mood; do not give in to it, for it will quickly cease. If you yield and leave this important and influential position, where you are free from petty annoyances and immune from the attacks of enemies, you may perhaps again experience its attraction and find difficulty in returning.'

"For almost six months beginning with July 1095 I was torn between the attraction of worldly desires and the summons of the world to come. In that month the matter ceased to be one of choice and became one of necessity. God parched my tongue and I was prevented from teaching. I would make an effort to teach one day for the sake of my audience, but my tongue would not utter a word. This impediment in speech produced grief in my heart; my digestion was affected, and I could hardly swallow anything. My general health declined, and the physicians, realizing that the source of the trouble was in the heart, despaired of successful treatment, unless the anxiety of the heart could be relieved.

"Aware of my impotence and without the power of choice, I took refuge with God, driven to do so because I had no resource left. He answered me, he 'who answers the one driven to him, when he calls on him' (Qur'ān 27. 62/63). He made it easy for my heart to turn from position, wealth, children and friends. I made public my decision to set out for Mecca, but my private plan was to travel to Syria, for I did not want the caliph and all my friends to learn of my decision to spend some time in Syria. This stratagem for leaving Baghdad I neatly carried out, and was resolved never to return.

"Among the religious leaders of Iraq there was much talk about me, for none thought it possible that my abandonment of everything could have a religious ground. Knowing no better, they considered that I had attained to the climax of a religious career. People in general were confused in their explanations. Those far from Iraq supposed I was apprehensive of ill-treatment by the rulers. Those close to the rulers, who observed how they sought me out and how I kept aloof from them, took the view that this was a supernatural affair, due to some evil influence which had come over the people of Islam and the circle of the scholars."

One important point in this account is that al-Ghazālī was dissatisfied with the subjects he was teaching. From his criticisms of the "religious sciences" in the first book of *The Revival* it would appear that he was thinking of the branches of jurisprudence chiefly cultivated at this time—and this is a ground for holding that he lectured on jurisprudence at least as much as on theology. Much attention was given to the study of the differences between the main legal rites and to the elaboration of sections of the Sharī'a or revealed law which were of little practical application. Such subjects undoubtedly gave men little help in leading a godly and upright life. In this al-Ghazālī was correct. What is surprising, however, is that he made no attempt to use his position and influence to have changes made in the curriculum. This at least is the natural reaction of a modern scholar, even when it is remembered that changes in the curriculum would be much more difficult in the age of al-Ghazālī. Further reflection, however, suggests other considerations. Perhaps al-Ghazālī felt that the whole system was so permeated by false values that a change in the curriculum, even if it could be effected, would be of little avail. He would presumably have liked to include the moral and devotional subjects of which he writes in *The Revival of the Religious Sciences*; but it might have been difficult to find people to lecture in these, and they would not have been adequate training for young lawyers.

His abandonment of any attempt to reform higher education is also connected with the second important point which appears in his account of the crisis—his distrust of his own motives. He felt he was in grave danger of hell, and this chiefly on account of his worldliness.

He would seem to have come to the conclusion that he personally, because of his temperament, was unable to be immersed in the life of the higher circles of Baghdadian society without becoming contaminated by the prevalent worldliness. He evidently did not feel that he was able, like his master al-Fārmadhī, to speak to the great ones about their faults. He was, of course, more involved in the system than al-Fārmadhī. He had practically the leading position among the intellectuals of Baghdad, and presumably maintained a standard of life in keeping with this position—and that in a world where the outward signs of status were reckoned important. Had he attempted to take an independent line in such circumstances, the result would certainly have been unfortunate. He would be unlikely to accomplish much, and he would gain ignominy for himself and hardships for his family. Freedom from worldly involvements seemed to be a necessary condition for any attempt to bring about a reform.

If it is thought that such an attitude shows undue concern for the welfare of a man's own soul at the expense of the welfare of society, it should be remembered that this attitude has deep roots in Islamic history. As early as the first century of Islam men began to have scruples about receiving payment from the rulers for services in judicial or legal matters. Originally—that is, in the days when all Muslims were receiving adequate stipends from the public treasury—such services seem to have been given without any special payment, and for long this was held up as an ideal. Some men went so far as to hold that such services should not be performed even without payment, since this degree of contact with worldly rulers was corrupting. Long before al-Ghazālī's time, however, it had become the usual practice for judges and similar officials to be paid. Yet the old ideal was not completely dead. Al-Masʿūdī (d. 956) tells of a man who, when he first knew him, accepted poverty gladly, but who later became a judge and completely changed in character for the worse.[22]

Two views have been put forward in recent times which give a somewhat different account from the above of the motives for al-Ghazālī's departure from Baghdad. At the turn of the century Duncan Black Macdonald made the suggestion that the withdrawal from teaching might have something to do with al-Ghazālī's being *persona non grata* with the sultan Barkiyāruq.[23] More recently Farid Jabre has argued with greater vehemence that the dominant motive was fear of being assassinated by the Bāṭinites.[24]

Macdonald's suggestion about the difficulties with Barkiyāruq was probably not intended to do more than call attention to a secondary factor, since he accepted al-Ghazālī's "conversion" to the mystic life as genuine. The chief arguments were the coincidence of dates and al-Ghazālī's implication in the recognition by the caliph of Barkiyāruq's rival Tutush for a time in 1094. It was in February 1095 that it became clear, with the death of Tutush, that Barkiyāruq was victor in the struggle with him (which had lasted since the death of Malikshāh in November 1092). Al-Ghazālī's illness began in July 1095, and he left Baghdad in November. Again, Barkiyāruq's death was in late December 1104, and it was some eighteen months later that al-Ghazālī returned to teaching at Nishapur. Because of this correspondence of dates, some causal connection cannot be ruled out. On the whole, however, it seems unlikely. In the tangled politics of the time, men frequently appeared to change sides. Barkiyāruq was generally on good terms with Fakhr-al-Mulk, a son of Niẓām-al-Mulk who had inherited something of his talents and his policies, and who was later responsible for al-Ghazālī's return to teaching at Nishapur. With this powerful support it is not credible that al-Ghazālī's trifling fault would have necessitated his departure from his post at Baghdad—and he himself asserts that he was courted by the rulers. There may be a grain of truth in the suggestion, however, in so far as the vicissitudes of the years after 1092 and the need for maintaining a delicate balance on the political tight-rope may have helped to convince al-Ghazālī that nothing of what he was interested in could be achieved through politics and his semi-political position in Baghdad.

Jabre's views, which to begin with appear to be an explanation of al-Ghazālī's departure from Baghdad, develop into an interpretation of his whole career. Of his dogmatic theology Jabre writes: "he thus repeated against the Bāṭinites what Ashʿarī had done two centuries earlier against the Muʿtazilites: starting from their own principles he rethought Sunnite dogma for himself and for his contemporaries". He even goes so far as to say: "from 486/1093 this (*sc.* the work of Ghazālī) had a single aim: to substitute, in the belief of his contemporaries, for the infallibility of the Bāṭinite imam that of the Prophet, the sole intermediary between God and man".[25] Now these are palpable exaggerations. It is true that al-Ghazālī sometimes speaks (as in *Deliverance from Error*) of Muḥammad as the infallible imam of the Muslims in general. But there is not a single section of his chief dogmatic work *The Golden Mean in Belief* that is seriously affected by this conception. The same is true of *The Revival of the Religious Sciences*; everywhere Muḥammad is the great exemplar, according to the usual Sunnite outlook, but nowhere is there an advance on this and an insistence on his infallibility as a source of knowledge. While the reaction to Bāṭinism may have contributed something to these works, it cannot have been more than a minor factor.

Even as an explanation of al-Ghazālī's outward

conduct fear of assassination by the Bāṭinites is not adequate. Jabre argues that, while al-Ghazālī may genuinely have felt that he was too worldly, this fault could have been corrected without leaving his position in Baghdad, and that therefore something further is required to explain his departure, and that this must be fear of imminent danger to his life.[26] Yet, even if it is admitted that such a fear may explain the departure from Baghdad, it does not explain why al-Ghazālī chose the life of a ṣūfī and cultivated mystical experience so assiduously; there were other ways open to him of becoming inconspicuous. Indeed, it is difficult to see how fear of assassination, which involves attaching greater importance to this world than to the world to come, could lead to al-Ghazālī's intensity in preparing for the world to come. Large tracts of his conduct are only to be explained by a genuine belief in the Last Judgement, and a man with a firm belief of this kind would not be afraid of death as such but only as reducing his time for preparing himself to be judged. If there was a real danger of his being assassinated, this must be how it affected al-Ghazālī. This is in accordance with a passage on which Jabre lays some emphasis, in which al-Ghazālī is reported to have spoken of "the opening of a door of fear";[27] but he went on to say, not that this caused him to leave Baghdad, but that it led him to fuller ascetical practices and deeper mystical experiences.

Whether there was any danger of assassination, such as Jabre supposes, must remain doubtful. Though Niẓām-al-Mulk had been assassinated in 1092, it is not clear that assassination had been adopted by the Bāṭinites as a regular practice before 1095; most of the examples come after that. It is also worth noticing that the danger was greater when al-Ghazālī returned to teaching in 1106, and that his new patron, Fakhr-al-Mulk, was assassinated a month or two after his return. It is further not clear that al-Ghazālī was the kind of person the Bāṭinites murdered—the caliph, for example, was surely in greater danger. One's respect for Jabre's arguments is not increased when one finds him, without any statement of reasons, disregarding accepted conclusions, such as Goldziher's dating of the *Mustaẓ'hirī* (his first book in refutation of the Bāṭinites) after *The Incoherence of the Philosophers*.[28] More serious is his interpretation of some statements that certain philosophical circles were attracted to Bāṭinism as implying that it was a section of the Bāṭinites who were attacked in *The Incoherence*; it should have been obvious that no philosophically-minded person can at the same time hold that truth is reached by syllogistic reasoning and by appeal to the pronouncements of an infallible imam.

It is important to see this matter in perspective. A perusal of the chronicles of the period by Ibn-al-Athīr makes it clear that there were many dangers threatening men in political life besides that from the Bāṭinites. There may have been some personal threat to al-Ghazālī from the Bāṭinites of which we know nothing; but even apart from this there was much to make him aware that life was precarious. A sense of the precariousness of his life, whatever its source and whatever its intensity, is not sufficient to account for all his intellectual and spiritual development, but it would certainly contribute to the growth of his dissatisfaction with the circumstances in which the intellectual of the time had to work and with the quality of life that was possible. This dissatisfaction is the key to al-Ghazālī's life; he expressly states it in the opening book of *The Revival*; and, as the present study is trying to show, he had good grounds for being dissatisfied.

3 LIFE AS A ṢŪFĪ

Before leaving Baghdad in November 1095 al-Ghazālī had made arrangements for the education of his children, partly, it would seem, from his own wealth, and partly from educational trusts which were numerous in Iraq. Doubtless he also made provision for his wife or wives, in so far as that was not already done in the marriage contract, but nothing is reported about this since in Islamic society it was impolite to mention wives. After this he gave away the remainder of his wealth, and thus committed himself to living the life of a poor ṣūfī.

In Damascus, where he first went, he says he spent "nearly two years", passing most of his time in solitude or retirement and engaging in devotional exercises. It was presumably a life similar to that which he describes in *The Beginning of Guidance*,[29] and which is based on a rule similar to that of Christian monastic communities. Many stories—most of them perhaps apocryphal—are told of his residence in Damascus. It seems likely, however, that he was unable to conceal his identity altogether, and that many serious-minded persons in Damascus took advantage of the presence of this great scholar among them. This may be why, in order to be alone, he would go up the minaret of the mosque at Damascus and shut himself in for the whole day.

In his own later account of this time[30] he says he went on to Jerusalem, and he must have spent some days or weeks there, engaged in solitary prayer and meditation in the Dome of the Rock, the site of Solomon's temple and the alleged site of Abraham's sacrifice of his son and of Muḥammad's miraculous night-journey to heaven. From Jerusalem he decided to make the pilgrimage to Mecca. On the way he prayed at the tomb of Abraham at Hebron and that of Muḥammad at Medina. "Then", his account continues, "my concerns and the appeals of my children drew me to my homeland, and I went back, after I had been the furthest of mortals from returning." He still cultivated solitude, but found it difficult to secure the peace he desired, for distractions were many.

Nevertheless, he persevered in his religious exercises, and always returned from his distractions to his quest for inner peace and illumination. At this stage he continued, he says, for ten years. A deeper understanding came to him of the principles of religion, and he was convinced that the way of life he was following was the truest and highest.

In this later autobiographical account there are many difficulties. From soon after his death there have been widely divergent views about the details of his movements. Some of the early biographical notices say that he spent ten years in Syria, having returned there after his pilgrimage to Mecca. Now it seems probable that he returned to Damascus, and that he regards his pilgrimage and his visit to Jerusalem as belonging to his Damascus period. This is in accordance with his account, provided that we take his phrase about the "journey to the Ḥijāz" to mean a journey to Mecca and back to Damascus; this seems to be a reasonable interpretation. It is practically certain, however, that he did not spend ten years at Damascus. His own words do not necessitate it; indeed, they suggest that he returned to his "homeland" not long after his pilgrimage; the word *thumma*, "then", seems to indicate an interval but not an unduly long one. He is reported to have made the pilgrimage in 489 (November–December 1096),[31] and also to have been encountered in Baghdad about June 1097.[32] There seems to be no ground for rejecting the first of these dates, and the second fits in well with most of the relevant facts. The chief remaining difficulty is that al-Ghazālī himself speaks of being "nearly two years" at Damascus, while, if we accept this second date, he cannot have been there more than eighteen months—from November 1095 to June 1097—even if the time spent on the pilgrimage is counted in; it seems best, however, to accept the date and to assume that al-Ghazālī used the phrase "nearly two years" somewhat loosely. His reference to "ten years" will then be to the whole time from his departure from Baghdad to his making arrangements for a return to teaching at Nishapur (which actually took place in July 1106). A subordinate reason for thinking he did not spend ten years in Damascus is that the activity of the Crusaders was beginning, Jerusalem falling to them in July 1099, and there are no signs of al-Ghazālī being affected by the Crusades.

It has often been asserted that he paid a visit to Egypt from Damascus. The dating which has just been argued for leaves time for only the briefest of visits. It is certainly possible that there was such a visit on the way to or from Mecca. If it took place, however, it can have been little more than an incident of the journey, and the absence of any mention of it in *Deliverance from Error* indicates that it had no spiritual significance for al-Ghazālī.

Another question which might be raised is what al-Ghazālī meant by "homeland" (*waṭan*). Was it Iraq or Khurasan? He spoke of the excellence of the educational trusts in Iraq in connection with his arrangements for his children. It is a generally accepted fact, however, that he spent some time in his native town of Ṭūs before returning to teaching at the not very distant Nishapur. Since he is not mentioned in the report of reactions in Baghdad to the fall of Jerusalem in 1099, it has been argued that he had already left.[33] Though this argument is not conclusive, it is likely that he went to Ṭūs about this time (passing through Hamadhān on the way),[34] for some of the biographers place a stay of several years in Ṭūs before his return to teaching in 1106. Here he lived a somewhat monastic life, but he also established a hostel or convent (*khanqāh*) and permitted disciples to share his life; he also discoursed to them on the subjects treated in *The Revival of the Religious Sciences*. The names are known of several men who became his disciples at Ṭūs.[35]

By way of summarizing the above discussions the following brief account of his movements from 1095 to 1106 might be given. On leaving Baghdad in November 1095 al-Ghazālī proceeded to Damascus and lived quietly there. Towards the end of 1096 he went to Jerusalem. During the months of November and December 1096 he was engaged in the pilgrimage, perhaps visiting Alexandria on the way. He went back to Damascus, but not later than June 1097 returned to Baghdad. He spent some time there, but possibly about 1099 returned to his native town of Ṭūs, and founded a small institution for the cultivation of the religious life. In 1105 or early in 1106 Fakhr-al-Mulk, the son of Niẓām-al-Mulk, who had now become vizier of the Seljūq prince Sanjar, governor of Khurasan, prevailed upon al-Ghazālī to accept a post—presumably the chief professorship—at the Niẓāmiyya college at Nishapur. There he took up his duties in July or August 1106. This was the eleventh month of the Islamic year 499; and al-Ghazālī was influenced by a Tradition to the effect that at the beginning of each century the Islamic community would have a "renewer" of religion, since his friends insisted that he was to be the "renewer" for the new century.[36]

There is not much more of the story to tell. Al-Ghazālī continued teaching at Nishapur for at least three years. A book on legal theory, commonly known as the *Mustaṣfā* and apparently containing his lectures at Nishapur, was completed in August 1109.[37] It was perhaps a little earlier that he wrote his autobiographical work, *Deliverance from Error*, since he was still teaching at Nishapur when he wrote it. At some date after August 1109 he once more gave up teaching and retired to his native town of Ṭūs. The reason for this retirement we can only conjecture. While personal difficulties of the kind which led to his withdrawal from Baghdad cannot be excluded, it is possible that he retired because of failing health and the beginning of the illness which led to his death on December 18th, 1111. It may well be that he did not return to Ṭūs until 1110 or early 1111; a reference to a man who studied law with him at Ṭūs seems to refer to this period, if the source has not confused Nishapur and Ṭūs.[38] Even if his retirement was due to ill-health he must still have been able to write, since he appears to have completed a small book less than a fortnight before he died.[39] On the day of his death, his brother Aḥmad related, he made his ablutions and performed the dawn worship; he then asked for his shroud, took it, kissed it and laid it on his eyes with the words, "Obediently I enter into the presence of the King"; then he stretched out his feet, faced the *qibla* (the direction of Mecca), and before daybreak was dead.[40]

The book he completed just before his death has the title, *The Restraining of the Commonalty from the Science of Theology*, and it is worth looking for a moment at its contents. It purports to be a reply to a questioner. "You have asked me about the Traditions which the ignorant and erring Ḥashwiyya (a sect or tendency) imagine to necessitate anthropomorphism; for they believe that God has a form, a hand, a mouth, a foot, that he comes down, moves his position, sits on the throne, and so on, in accordance with the literal meaning of the Traditions; they also claim that their belief is that of the fathers (*salaf*); so you want me to explain what is the belief of the fathers and to show what the ordinary man must believe about these Traditions."[41] The first chapter deals with the true position of the fathers concerning the Traditions in question, and maintains that according to the fathers the ordinary man has seven duties with regard to these anthropomorphic conceptions: he must realize that they do not imply that God is corporeal; he must believe them since they come from God (in the case of Qur'ānic conceptions) or from Muḥammad; he must realize his own inability to understand them positively; he must not ask about them, or try to explain them by using other words, or even puzzle over them in his own mind, but must accept the views of those who have knowledge of such matters. The second chapter deals with the truth of the doctrine of the fathers, and proves it both by reason and from Tradition; the general rational proof makes the following points: the Prophet was best informed about the position of man with regard to the future life; he passed on to mankind all that was revealed to him; the closest Companions were best informed about the meaning of his words; these discouraged men from investigating the conceptions further. The third chapter deals with miscellaneous questions, ending up with a statement of the six grades of belief: belief after strict proof, complete at every step; belief after proof based on premisses not strictly proved but generally accepted by scholars; belief based on rhetorical proofs; belief in the statement of a trustworthy person; belief in a statement made in circumstances generally accepted as satisfactory; belief in a statement because one wants to believe it without considering if the informant is trustworthy.

There is much in this little book which is worthy of careful study, and all that can be done here is to notice some points relevant to present concerns. Firstly, it is directed against people whom al-Ghazālī calls Ḥashwiyya, and these are presumably Ḥanbalites and Traditionists,[42] and perhaps also the Karrāmites. Secondly, one of the main concerns of the book is to avoid anthropomorphism (*tashbīh*) or the literal interpretation of such expressions as "the hand of God"; yet at the same time al-Ghazālī wants ordinary men to accept these expressions with simple faith without engaging in rational discussion of them. This is his programme of a *via media* which he sketches briefly in *The Niche for Lights*;[43] he seeks to avoid a literal interpretation which implies corporeality in God and an allegorical interpretation which abandons the scriptural conception. Thirdly, the book is presumably directed to scholars and theologians, and there is no suggestion of a degree of understanding beyond theirs, though nothing to exclude various levels of understanding among them.

It is important to notice these points. It is still often stated or assumed that there was a closing phase in al-Ghazālī's life when he abandoned Ashʿarism and became a Neoplatonist. This book, completed a few days before his death, shows him thinking and arguing essentially as an Ashʿarite; even if he had earlier gone beyond Ashʿarism in some of his speculations (such as those about the nature of prophethood and the "immediate experience" of the mystics), he has not abandoned any Islamic dogma or any of the central positions of Ashʿarism. From this it follows that works of a Neoplatonic character ascribed to al-Ghazālī must be regarded as spurious. The only possible exception to this is, if it can be shown that a specific work was written between about 1091 and 1096, which is the time when his enthusiasm for philosophy was greatest. To this period belongs a work on ethics mainly from the standpoint of Greek philosophy which is genuine at least in part, but to which he never refers in his later books[44]—presumably because he came to think about ethical questions more in traditional Islamic terms. That any other of the works of doubtful authenticity can be ascribed to him at this period has not yet been shown. The careful study of dates by Maurice Bouyges, however, seems to have cut the ground from the idea that he turned to Neoplatonism in his closing years. Even the tendency to treat ordinary men differently from scholars—which might suggest that he was concealing esoteric views—is to be found in his thoroughly Ashʿarite work on dogmatics, *The Golden Mean in Belief*.[45]

4 "THE REVIVAL OF THE RELIGIOUS SCIENCES"

It is universally acknowledged that al-Ghazālī's greatest work is *The Revival of the Religious Sciences*. It is by far the lengthiest, usually occupying four volumes of some fifteen hundred large pages. A complete English translation would probably have at least two million words. This great work belongs to his period as a ṣūfī. A small part of it, known as *The Epistle from Jerusalem*, was probably composed separately during his visit to Jerusalem in 1096, and it may be that the work as a whole was not conceived till later. He would require time to settle down after the crisis of 1095 before he could contemplate such a work. It doubtless took several years to compose, though it has to be remembered that Arabic can be written almost as fast as shorthand and that al-Ghazālī appears to have been a fast worker. Various literary problems connected with it have not yet been adequately studied—whether it was written in order as it stands, or whether some portions (such as the beginning of the third quarter) are later additions; how it is related to the shorter abbreviation known as *The Book of the Forty* and to the longer Persian abridgement, *The Alchemy of Happiness*. Clearly any attempt to assess al-Ghazālī's achievement must pay considerable attention to this work.

The Revival is divided into four "quarters", and each of these into ten books.[46] The first quarter is entitled "matters of service (*sc.* of God)" or, as we might say, "cult practices". The first book, as has been mentioned earlier, deals with knowledge or science, and is doubtless intended as an introduction to the whole. The seven chapters into which it is divided deal with a number of different topics, but the main concern is to indicate which subjects of study or "sciences" are of importance for a devout Muslim, and in what measure. In various places there occur the criticisms of the scholar-jurists of the day, which have already been noted. The second book is about the basic principles of the creed, and contains: (*a*) an elaboration of the Confession of Faith—"I bear witness that there is no god but God, Muḥammad is the Messenger of God"; (*b*) a discussion of education in matters of doctrine; (*c*) a statement of Islamic doctrine in four sections, each with ten points; (*d*) a discussion of the relation between faith and Islam, that is, between being a believer and being a Muslim. In one sense this is still introductory material, but in another sense the Confession of Faith might be regarded as a cult practice.

The remaining eight books of the first quarter deal with: ritual purity (ablutions before worship, etc.), formal prayers or worship, tithing, fasting, the pilgrimage to Mecca, the recitation of the Qur'ān, private prayer, and supererogatory and extracanonical devotions. Each practice is usually introduced by Qur'ānic verses and Traditions justifying it, and by sayings of Muḥammad and devout Muslims advocating and praising it. How to carry it out is explained in very great detail—some of this can be very surprising to Western students not accustomed to a legalistic outlook in matters of religious practice. Al-Ghazālī, however, is always concerned not merely that a man's external practice should be flawless, but that he should also have the appropriate inner attitudes and understand something of the deeper reasons for what he does. In short, al-Ghazālī looks upon the external practices as means by which a man becomes "near to God" and prepares himself for the life of the world to come.

The second quarter is entitled "customs" and deals with the external aspects of ordinary life outside the practice of the cult. For the Muslim practically all the matters dealt with come within the sphere of the revealed law or Sharīʿa, though we should classify some as ethical, some as legal and some as questions of etiquette. There are books about eating and drinking, marriage, earning one's living and engaging in business, relations with friends and relatives, the life of retirement, travelling, and the use of music. One book entitled "Of the lawful and unlawful" is really about questions of conscience. Another might be said to be about reforming society and improving its tone. The last book is a word-picture of Muḥammad as the exemplar of all the qualities extolled in the earlier books. Though there is much "secular" detail in this quarter, al-Ghazālī never loses sight of the contribution of the things he discusses to man's spiritual growth.

The last two quarters deal explicitly with man's inner life, and are entitled respectively "things leading to destruction" and "things leading to salvation" or, as we might say "vices" and "virtues". The first book of the third quarter is an introductory account of "the mysteries of the heart", and is followed by a book dealing with the improvement of the character in a general way. Then come books on the control of the appetites for food and sexual intercourse, on the weaknesses of the tongue, on anger, on worldliness, on avarice, on hypocrisy and love of fame, on pride and vanity, and on self-deception. The books of the fourth quarter are respectively on repentance, on patience and gratitude (to God), on fear and hope, on poverty and self-discipline, on asserting God's unity and trusting in him, on love (for God) and approval (of his decrees), on sincerity and purity of intention, on self-examination, on meditation, and on death and the life to come. Thus the second half of *The Revival* is not unlike many Christian devotional manuals and spiritual guides, such as the *Introduction to the Devout Life* of Saint François de Sales.

The importance of all this is that it shows us that for al-Ghazālī ṣūfism meant much more than the cultivation of ecstatic states. He was constantly aware of this life as a preparation for the life to come. Since the prelude of the life to come was the Last Judgement, he was very much concerned with the improvement of character. Though he had some experience of mystical ecstasy, he appears never to have sought this for its own sake but only as supporting and facilitating the improvement of character and as leading to a higher degree of reward in the life to come (since he believed in degrees of reward in Paradise). This is very relevant to the assessment of his achievement.

VII

THE INTELLECTUAL BASIS OF THE "REVIVED" COMMUNITY

INTRODUCTORY NOTE

Any attempt to discuss the whole range of al-Ghazālī's thought in *The Revival of the Religious Sciences* would lead too far away from the specific concern of the present study. It seems possible, however, to isolate certain points which are relevant to the place and function of the class of intellectuals in Islamic society. Since part of what al-Ghazālī does is to suggest the conception of a new and higher kind of knowledge, it will be necessary to look again at the relations of Islamic conceptions of knowledge to the class of intellectuals.

VII

THE INTELLECTUAL BASIS OF THE "REVIVED" COMMUNITY

I THE INTELLECTUAL CLASS AND THE CONCEPTION OF KNOWLEDGE

ONE of the general principles underlying this book is that there is a parallelism between the function of the intellectual class in society and the function of intellect in the life of the individual and of society. The ideas which the intellect employs help to direct our activity, both when we are responding to a change in the circumstances of our lives and when we are maintaining a steady way of life in stable circumstances.[1] In general, the intellectuals are the bearers of the ideas through which a society directs its activity. They ensure that the ideas are transmitted from generation to generation, and remain operative in the society. Where there are outward changes in the life of a society, it is usually desirable that there should be an ideational change to direct the fresh adjustments of practice to the changed circumstances. Sometimes, in societies where there is an official intellectual class, it may happen that this class has become insensitive to the impact of changed circumstances on the ordinary man and that it fails to make the necessary adaptation of ideas; in such a case attempts will be made by persons outside the intellectual class to adapt the ideation of the society. There is, of course, no necessity that the attempts to modify and adapt ideas should be successful, whether made by official intellectuals or by others. A process of trial and error, sometimes lengthy, is usually required before a satisfactory modification of ideas is found. What is true is that, until a satisfactory modification is found, men are dissatisfied with life in their society, and this dissatisfaction exerts a constant pressure to seek more adequate ideation.

It has usually been found in practice that it is desirable that the intellectuals should be a distinct and autonomous class. This is in contrast to Plato, who thought that in the ideal state there should be a single class of philosopher-kings, combining the functions of rulers and intellectuals. The weaknesses of human nature, however, seem to exclude this. The ruler who is also the bearer of ideation is constantly under the temptation to modify the ideation in order to facilitate his own immediate problems in ruling, regardless of the long-term interests of the society as a whole.[2] Ideally, it would seem, the ruling institution and the intellectuals should be parallel, and the intellectuals should be autonomous, that is, able to formulate their ideational systems independently of the rulers, or at least without undue pressure from the rulers. At the same time, of course, the ideational systems must be relevant to the interests and problems of the rulers. A proper balance between rulers and intellectuals is always difficult to achieve. Many of the troubles of the Islamic world can be traced to the rulers' domination of the intellectuals and the latter's subservience to the rulers.

That the life of a society is directed by its ideas is a fact, whatever theory the society holds about the nature and function of ideas. Yet theories about ideas or about knowledge have a certain influence on the life of the society—and most actual theories are very inadequate accounts of the complexity of the phenomena. Thus, for a time sections of Western society took the naïve view that men acted according to a set of "rational" ideas, until experience showed that this was often not the case; then certain sections rushed to the opposite error of thinking that ideas had no influence at all on actual life. Through all this, however, the ideation of Western society has been fulfilling the normal function of ideation in a society.

In Islamic society the development of the intellectual class has been influenced in detail by the specific Islamic or perhaps rather Arabic conception of knowledge (*'ilm*). Knowledge is thought of as being contained in propositions formulated by outstanding men. In earlier days there were wise men and poets; then came the prophet Muḥammad. The knowledge contained in these propositions is handed on by the simple transmission of the words in the propositions. This need not be taken to imply that there is nothing beyond the words, or that someone who can repeat the words perfectly has fully entered into the knowledge or wisdom of those who first formulated the propositions. It may be held that there is something beyond the words, but this can only be reached by meditating on the words. If this is so, knowledge cannot altogether be transmitted, but such transmission of it as is possible is effected by transmitting the form of words in which it was originally expressed. It follows that the handing on of the knowledge or ideation which is the basis of the Islamic community is achieved by learning by heart the Qur'ān and the Traditions about the sayings and acts of Muḥammad. Great insistence will be placed on verbal accuracy, even in respect of secondary reporters of Traditions. Thus the Arabic-Islamic conception of knowledge colours the whole of Islamic education.

A corollary of this conception of knowledge is that the only real knowledge is that of a few outstanding men. In respect of essential religious matters Muḥammad is, for the Islamic community, the last of such outstanding men, and it has, therefore, no knowledge subsequent to the Qur'ān and the Traditions, except in the peripheral spheres of legal and mystical conceptions. This seems to be a reflection of the static character of Arabian tribal society. There the highest wisdom was in keeping to the "beaten path" or *sunna* trodden by one's ancestors.

This conception of Muḥammad as having given the latest and fullest expression of wisdom available to Islamic man made it difficult for the intellectuals to adapt Islamic ideation to the rapidly changing circumstances of the nascent Islamic empire. Indeed, they could only perform their function by pretending that they were not making changes. Despite this handicap they performed the stupendous task of adapting the ideation originally designed for the little state of Muḥammad's lifetime to the needs of a vast empire. This result was achieved by adapting or inventing sayings of Muḥammad, and then developing a critique of such sayings to distinguish "sound" Traditions from unsound. By about 850 a corpus of "sound" Traditions had been formed and stabilized; in effect, "sound" meant what was appropriate to the circumstances of the ninth-century empire and was approved by the main body of intellectuals. The fictive idea that all this came from Muḥammad was universally accepted, and the conception of the unchanging character of Islamic knowledge thereby given deeper roots. Up to this point the achievement of the intellectuals was impressive, but they had made it even more difficult for their successors to adapt Islamic ideation to the needs of later centuries. It was no longer to be possible to invent fresh sayings of Muḥammad, for the corpus of "sound" Traditions had been closed. Ingenuity could still find ways of making ideational modifications, but the difficulties were greater, and so it was more likely that there would be failures to achieve satisfactory modifications.

While the corpus of Traditions was reaching stability,

a new and complicating element appeared, Greek philosophy. This has already been discussed from various angles in this book, but it may now be looked on from a fresh perspective, as a new conception of the nature of knowledge. Part of the interest in Greek philosophy among Muslims rose from the need to defend Islamic doctrine against non-Muslims, and in particular against Christian inhabitants of the caliphate who had received a philosophical training. Against such persons arguments based on the Qur'ān and Traditions were useless; first of all, reasons had to be given for accepting the authority of these scriptures. This led to the development of a great work of apologetics at various levels, for arguments had always to be based on what the opponents were prepared to accept or concede. Out of such apologetics arose a new conception of knowledge. It seemed clear that the man who could give reasons for a doctrine he believed was superior to a man who merely held the doctrine, but could give no reasons for it. The former came to be the knower or man of knowledge *par excellence*—*'ālim*, plural *'ulamā'*, participle used as a noun from the root of *'ilm*, knowledge; it is anglicized as *ulema*, and rendered in this book by "scholar-jurists". Naturally there was resistance to this new conception of knowledge. The philosophical or rational theology incorporating it, known as *kalām*, was accepted by many theologians (known as *mutakallimūn*) and jurists. The chief group of those who opposed eventually came to be the Ḥanbalites, the followers of the legal rite of Aḥmad ibn-Ḥanbal.

In the two hundred years or so between the stabilization of Tradition and the student days of al-Ghazālī the ideational system of Islam had become ossified, and, parallel to this, something had gone wrong with the class of intellectuals. It would be rash to attempt a final pronouncement on matters which have not been fully investigated, but suggestions may be made about factors which may have contributed to the end-result.

(*a*) The conception of knowledge (or ideation) as static, as just noted, made it difficult for the intellectuals to effect ideational changes explicitly. It seems probable, too, that several groups of people had an interest in maintaining the pretence that nothing had changed. The war-lords who came to rule the lands of the caliphate during this period were content with the actuality of power, and may have thought that it made retention of power easier if the masses still regarded the caliph as supreme. The caliph and his supporters, too, were probably anxious to keep in being a semblance of the old system, in the hope that one day the caliph might sally out from this bastion to recover the power he had lost.

(*b*) The great increase in the extent of the ideational basis of Islamic society and the corresponding increase in the time required to gain a mastery of it meant that the class of intellectuals had become more of a closed corporation. There still seem to have been lectures in mosques which anyone might attend; but the young man who wanted to make a career for himself as an intellectual and rise to a judgeship or professorship had to study hard for many years and also to travel widely so as to sit under some of the most distinguished scholars. Thus the intellectuals tended to be more marked off from ordinary men, and to be a little jealous of their privileges as a distinct group. They also tended to be much concerned with advancement within the series of posts open to them, to study those parts of learning in which they could show off to their fellows their intellectual abilities, and in general to have a worldly outlook.

(*c*) The tendency to worldliness was strengthened by the weakness of the intellectuals as a class over against the rulers. This goes back at least to the Inquisition of 833–849,[3] where it had been demonstrated that only a handful of intellectuals were prepared to resist coercion by the rulers. Under the Buwayhid sultans or war-lords, who were Shīʿites, the position of the mainly Sunnite intellectuals was even less attractive. It is likely that their growing interest in external and worldly rewards was in part a compensation for their declining importance in the community.

(*d*) The greater "intellectualism", or more academic attitude, of the intellectuals is perhaps more a reflection of the above factors than an independent factor parallel to them. Intellectual elaboration where there are no foreseeable practical consequences is a way in which the intellectual finds compensation for frustration in his efforts in other directions. Such intellectualism may also be called scholastic in the sense that it is based on concepts derived by a process of abstraction from the living experience of an earlier generation without being filled out by reference to fresh contemporary experience.

While these four factors suggest something of what was happening to the intellectuals in the tenth and eleventh centuries new insights were developing outside the official intellectual class among the ṣūfīs or mystics. To be exact, a number of the ṣūfīs were members of the official intellectual class; but they had to regard their discipline as a new one to be cultivated privately, as it were, and not added to the official curriculum. Such at least is the general impression given by the sources, though the matter requires further investigation. It would seem, too, that it was because of the stability of Tradition and the difficulty of introducing modifications that ṣūfism had to be treated as something *new* and not a modification of something old. The Islamic mind is fond of dividing things into categories and treating of each category in isolation; and this habit of mind appears to have been used to make a place for the insights of ṣūfism in the intellectual life of Islam.

Ṣūfism was only new, of course, as a distinct discipline, parallel to theology, jurisprudence and the other "Islamic sciences"—a kind of extra in which a man might specialize if he so desired. In itself it claimed to be founded on Qur'ān and Tradition. Unfortunately its subject-matter was not such as to be kept in a watertight compartment; its ethics, for example, frequently overlapped the ethical aspects of the Sharīʿa, which were also the concern of jurisprudence. This was one of the problems al-Ghazālī tried to solve.

2 THE NEW "INTELLECTUAL STRUCTURE" OF THE COMMUNITY

Since al-Ghazālī's chief work is *The Revival of the Religious Sciences*, it is important for an appreciation of his whole career to know what he meant by "revival". From his criticisms of the official intellectuals we have learned that he regarded the religious sciences, as these were expounded in his time, as contributing very little to a man's attainment of future bliss; and this last he assumed to be the true end of human life. The sciences were being pursued in an academic fashion that was out of touch with the needs of the ordinary man in the contemporary world. Al-Ghazālī was therefore trying to rescue the sciences from this condition. What, in effect, he does in the earlier part of *The Revival* is to show that the prescriptions of the Sharīʿa, taken in considerable detail, can be made the foundation of a meaningful life, that is, as he sees it, a life of preparation for the world to come. This general conception is also expounded more briefly in various books written subsequently to *The Revival*, as already noted, and there are strong reasons for thinking that al-Ghazālī maintained this general position to the end of his life.

To speak of making the system of ideas and practices

of which the official intellectual class were the bearers relevant to contemporary needs involves a certain assumption, namely, an assessment of contemporary needs in accordance with the ṣūfistic outlook. This emphasized the individual's pursuit of uprightness as the supreme end in life, since in this way he attained to the bliss of Paradise, which was his ultimate end. At the same time there was implicit in the ṣūfistic outlook an abandonment of the attempt to make the whole society an upright society—except in so far as the society was changed by the force of the example of the ṣūfīs. Once much of the texture of social life was fixed by a stabilized Sharīʿa, and once political life was largely determined either by an autocratic caliph and his court (following the principles of Persian statecraft) or by war-lords pursuing their own interests, the ordinary man required to have some such religious aim set before him. The failure of the official bearers of religious truth was that they did not see this, while the fresh insight of the ṣūfīs was precisely this. The ṣūfīs, however, even when they were members of the official intellectual class and lectured on such subjects as jurisprudence, seem to have kept their ṣūfism in a separate compartment. Al-Qushayrī (d. 1072 in Ṭūs), though a Shāfiʿite jurist, in his well-known *Epistle on Ṣūfism* covers only the ground of the second half of *The Revival* and has no discussion of the matters in the first half. It is a distinctive feature of the work of al-Ghazālī that he links up the details of the Sharīʿa with the insights of the ṣūfīs.

As a result of his efforts in this direction al-Ghazālī comes to hold a doctrine of three possible intellectual or cognitive conditions in which a man may be. The lowest is that of faith (*īmān*), and at this stage a man accepts the doctrines of the creed on the authority of other persons, such as parents and teachers. This *taqlīd* or "following the authority of others" may also be described as "naïve belief", since the man may not be aware of his dependence on others, and may not have thought of asking how he comes to believe what he believes. (There are other instances—in law and in Bāṭinite theory—where *taqlīd* is conscious.) The second degree is that of knowledge or science (*'ilm*), where a man is able to give reasons for what he believes. This is the degree of the scholar-jurists or ulema, the official intellectual class; and it is in line with al-Ghazālī's criticisms of them that he places them in the middle degree and not in the highest. The third and highest degree in the usual account is that of insight or immediate experience (*dhawq*, literally "taste"), and it is here of course that the ṣūfīs are placed.[4]

It was apparently only gradually that al-Ghazālī came to place immediate experience above rational knowledge. There are passages in *The Revival* where he seems to suggest that immediate experience and academic (rational) study are parallel roads to truth, leading to the *same* result. Thus he writes: "The knowledge of the method of employing and profiting from (*sc.* such knowledge as one already has) sometimes comes through a divine light in the heart arising from the natural disposition, as in the case of the prophets . . . and sometimes —and this is more usual—comes from study and discipline".[5] This comes from Book 39 on "Meditation"; and it is perhaps significant that this material is not represented in the *Book of the Forty*, although that is approximately a summary of *The Revival*, divided into forty sections corresponding roughly to the forty books of the latter. On the other hand, the conception of the three levels—faith, knowledge, and immediate experience—is clearly formulated in the *Book of the Forty*.[6] It would seem, therefore, that al-Ghazālī slowly approached this conception of the three grades in the course of writing *The Revival*; but that, once he had clearly formulated it, he clung to it. It was doubtless the reflection of his own deepening mystical experiences, in which he came to feel that he now understood things he had not properly understood before.

The conception of the three grades implied that there was a class above that of the scholar-jurists or official intellectuals. This was the view of the ṣūfīs themselves at least as early as the time of Abū-Naṣr as-Sarrāj (d. 988),[7] who spoke of three groups of people—worldlings, religious and elect; although these are not the same as al-Ghazālī's three groups, they likewise imply the superiority of the ṣūfīs. An extreme expression of this belief in the superiority of the ṣūfīs is to be seen in the doctrine that at any given time the most saintly ṣūfī is the *quṭb* or axis who supports the whole order of the universe, so that without him it would be destroyed.[8] While al-Ghazālī did not go so far as to advocate that the ṣūfīs should be "officially" recognized as an intellectual class above the scholar-jurists—such recognition would have seemed to him an undesirable concession to worldliness—he gave them new and solid reasons for thinking they were such a superior class, namely, in their possession of a superior function. They have the immediate experience which gives insight, and their insight is the highest ideational guide of the community.

In a sense there is also implicit in al-Ghazālī's conception of the three grades an acknowledgement of the existence of a source of wisdom later in time than Muḥammad and capable of producing modifications of Islamic ideation suited to bringing about an adaptation to contemporary circumstances. Though this is implicit, however, al-Ghazālī himself was unaware of the implication. Far from asserting it explicitly he repeatedly insisted (chiefly against the Bāṭinites) that Muḥammad was the supreme fount of wisdom for the community. Most of the jurists held that adaptation of the Sharīʿa to contemporary situations was to be achieved by intellectual "effort" in accordance with rational principles. Ṣūfistic insights, however, were effecting adaptation at a deeper level, and al-Ghazālī's conception, though he did not realize the fact, was a justification of a change that was already taking place and which he himself brought to a consummation.

This "blind spot" is an indication of the extent to which he had failed to work out fully his conception of immediate experience. It has already been noted how he hesitated before asserting that immediate experience was above rational knowledge. There is, of course, a distinction between the two which is familiar to modern philosophers and which is expressed by al-Ghazālī with his usual clarity in *Deliverance from Error*.[9] It is the distinction between "knowledge about" and "acquaintance with" or "experience of". A man, as he puts it, may have complete scientific knowledge of what health is and what drunkenness is; but that is different from having experience of health and experience of drunkenness by being healthy and drunk respectively. Questions are begged, however, when this distinction is applied to the knowledge of God. Is it possible to have knowledge about God (as distinct from a knowledge of what *people say* about God) without having some experience of God? If a man, through faith in a prophet's message, has in some measure "entered into" the experience of (the reality apprehended by) the prophet, has he not to some extent had an experience of God? Again, why should "knowledge about" be considered inferior? Is the man with knowledge about drunkenness not superior to the drunk man? Is the man with a scientific (or philosophical) knowledge of the nature of sense-perception not superior to the man who perceives things without knowing what he is doing? Al-Ghazālī, as suggested above, seems to have generalized from his own experiences without realizing how many other questions were involved.

It would seem, for example, that in placing "immediate experience" above "knowledge", al-Ghazālī was presupposing that the persons who had "immediate experience" already possessed a large measure of "knowledge". This was so in so far as ṣūfīs came from the class of scholar-jurists, as al-Ghazālī himself and many leading ṣūfīs of the previous age had done. It seems likely, however, that among the crowds of corrupt ṣūfīs of whom we hear[10] there was little higher education and even very sketchy acquaintance with what al-Ghazālī expected ordinary men to hold by "faith". Would al-Ghazālī have placed the "immediate experience" of an uneducated ṣūfī above the knowledge of a jurist? We who observe how wild religious enthusiasts have been in recent centuries would be hesitant about this. Al-Ghazālī had the possibility of looking at the heresiography of al-Baghdādī (d. 1037), but it may not have occurred to him to place the assertions of extreme sectaries on the same level as the ecstasies of the mystics. Yet there is a real problem here. So far as the outward form of the experience goes—that is, so far as it is accessible to the uncommitted observer—there is nothing to show that the insight of the ṣūfī saint is more true than the imaginings of the erratic visionary. In other words, "immediate experience" requires a rational (or theological) critique.

Al-Ghazālī's failure to deal with this problem is linked with his failure to appreciate the function of the Sharīʿa in the life of the community. He appreciated it, of course, in insisting that the observance of the Sharīʿa must be the basis of the ṣūfistic life. Yet he does not fully realize that, while ṣūfistic insight gives a deeper meaning to the prescriptions of the Sharīʿa and shows the inner spirit which ought to inform the observance of them, it is not itself the source of these prescriptions. They are in a sense prior even to the ethical teaching of the ṣūfīs. Because of this priority these prescriptions are properly the subject-matter of an independent discipline—the "science" or "knowledge" of the scholar-jurists. This deals essentially with the outward form of the social structure of the community, that form with which the ordinary man must have some acquaintance by "faith", and of which the scholar has fuller, more precise and more systematic "knowledge". The "immediate experience" of the ṣūfī is not related to the "knowledge" of the scholar as the latter is related to the "faith" of the ordinary man; it is a different kind of relationship. Perhaps al-Ghazālī failed to realize the problem here because, although much of his thinking was communalistic, his conception of "immediate experience" was still largely influenced by the individualistic thinking of the earlier ṣūfism. In essence what he fails to consider is how mystical experience is to become and remain relevant to the life of a community with a fixed social structure.

To sum up. Al-Ghazālī was striving to give expression to changes that had been taking place in Islamic life. In insisting (as in the first half of *The Revival*) that a life according to the Sharīʿa was the necessary basis of the ṣūfistic life, he was carrying a process of adaptation to its completion. In his conception of "immediate experience" he had isolated the new factor which had appeared in the Islamic world, especially after the stabilization of Tradition about 850, and was the source of the subsequent process of adaptation; but he had not been successful in his theoretic account of the factor, and he did not realize the need for controlling it.

VIII
THE ACHIEVEMENT

INTRODUCTORY NOTE

To assess the achievement of al-Ghazālī is no easy matter. He undoubtedly had considerable influence in succeeding centuries, but scholars have paid little attention to the centuries between his death and the beginnings of the European impact. What is to be said here can therefore be no more than a tentative and provisional estimate of his achievement. It is based on the perusal of a few well-known works and on some obvious historical facts, but may require emendation when the various periods have been more fully studied.

VIII
THE ACHIEVEMENT

I THE TENSION BETWEEN PHILOSOPHY AND THEOLOGY

It was seen in an earlier chapter that the tension between theology and philosophy which al-Ghazālī experienced was in part the rivalry of different groups of men, though behind this rivalry was the question of the relation between reason and revelation, between logical and intuitive knowledge. By making a thorough study of philosophy al-Ghazālī was seeking to resolve this tension by deliberately exposing himself more fully to it. While other theologians kept it at arm's length as something foreign and dangerous, or tried to attack it without understanding it, al-Ghazālī made a thorough study of it to discover the elements of strength and truth in it and to see whether these could be employed in the service of Sunnite Islam. He was only able to appreciate such elements, however, because he approached it with open-mindedness, that is, a readiness to abandon his Ash'arite theology for Neoplatonic philosophy, should he be convinced of the truth of the latter. The result of his activity was considerable and had both a positive and a negative aspect.

By the negative aspect is to be understood the weakening of the movement of pure philosophy. It might be thought that this could be regarded as the consequence of al-Ghazālī's book, *The Inconsistency of the Philosophers*; but this is one of the points which should not be assumed without further study. It is certain that in the heartlands of Islam, from Egypt to beyond the Oxus, there was no great name in philosophy after Ibn-Sīnā; but Ibn-Sīnā died in 1037, so that it is possible that pure philosophy was in decline before al-Ghazālī's attack on it. While what he attacked is not to be identified with any philosophy cultivated by the Ismā'īlites or Bāṭinites, it may well be that persons who had formerly professed themselves to be philosophers now turned to Ismā'īlism. Philosophy continued to be studied in the Islamic West, and outstanding philosophers appeared like Ibn-Ṭufayl and Ibn-Rushd (Averroes), who replied to the attacks of al-Ghazālī. How effective their replies were need not be decided here. Philosophy eventually declined in the Islamic West also, after passing on something of its spirit to Europe; but this decline is due more to the general decline of Islamic culture following on the resurgence of Christian Spain than to theological attacks. There is indeed some irony in the fact that al-Ghazālī was best known in medieval Europe for the exposition of the views of the Neoplatonists which he wrote as a preliminary to his *Inconsistency*.

If it is thus impossible to say how much al-Ghazālī's attacks contributed to the decline of philosophy, there is no doubt about the success of the positive aspects of his work, namely, the incorporation of parts of philosophy into Islamic theology. From this time onwards the theologians (apart from those who rejected rational argument, notably the Ḥanbalites) made use of syllogistic logic and various Greek metaphysical conceptions. Some of the later Ḥanbalites even felt themselves constrained to study syllogistic logic in order to refute it.[1] Theological treatises came to have large introductory sections on logic and metaphysics, and—more interesting—books on logic came to be written by theologians and not philosophers. In all this al-Ghazālī was the pioneer. The way may have been prepared for him by other men such as his teacher, al-Juwaynī. The times may have been ripe for a move in this direction. Yet al-Ghazālī alone made that combined study of philosophy and theology that was necessary if the tension was to be resolved, and endured the brunt of conservative disapproval and criticism. For his perspicacity and courage in this he deserves the fullest credit.

A charge that might perhaps be brought against him is that by thus making theology philosophical he contributed to its ossification or rigidification.[2] That theology became devitalized is clear. It is almost as clear that this devitalization went along with a growth of the philosophical element. Once again, however, this is a point requiring further study. There is no justification for thinking that philosophy itself is a devitalizing agent. The source of the trouble must be in the people who philosophize. Now these are the same class of religious intellectuals whose worldliness al-Ghazālī criticized. The first place to look for the cause of devitalization will therefore be among the attitudes of this class. Perhaps they were led to excess in philosophizing by the same motives which led them to excessive study of the "differences" between the legal rites. Al-Ghazālī, the vigorous critic of this form of study, cannot be blamed for the later development of a similar vice, even if he helped to provide the material for it.

2 THE BĀṬINITE CHALLENGE

Although al-Ghazālī gives some prominence in his autobiography to his refutations of Bāṭinite views, this side of his literary production was probably a secondary matter for him. His study of Bāṭinism taught him something about various aspects of Islamic life, and brought certain emphases into his doctrinal formulations (as in his insistence that Muḥammad is the inspired leader of the community); but it did not entail the same personal involvement as did his study of philosophy, since there is no sign that he was ever in any way tempted to become a Bāṭinite.

Whether his attacks on Bāṭinism made an important contribution to the decline and defeat of the movement is difficult to determine. On the whole the decline would seem to be chiefly due to many other factors—the decreasing support from the Fāṭimids in Egypt, and their failure to produce in Egypt a state of affairs notably different from that in the lands which acknowledged the ʿAbbāsid caliph, the domination of the movement by mountaineers and other relatively primitive elements of the population and a consequent alienation of the urban masses, and perhaps increasing contentedness under the firm rule of the Seljūqs. The fact that the movement had to resort to the assassination of the vizier Niẓām-al-Mulk in 1092 might betoken the desperation of a man who suspects he has failed. If that is so, then the Bāṭinite movement was declining before al-Ghazālī wrote a word about it. In any case the general function of polemical writings such as those in question is not to persuade the opponent of his folly, but to prevent further waverers on one's own side going over to him. In so far as al-Ghazālī's books gave confidence in themselves and in their own cause to the supporters of the ʿAbbāsids and the Seljūqs, they were a part, indeed a necessary part, of the efforts of the government against the rebels, and thus a necessary part of the defence of Sunnite Islam.

3. THE TENSION BETWEEN THE "ISLAMIC SCIENCES" AND ṢŪFISM

Great as was the service al-Ghazālī performed for Islam in exposing himself to the tension between philosophy and theology, it was surpassed—it is generally held—by what he achieved by exposing himself deliberately to the further tension between the ṣūfistic movement and the established "Islamic sciences". Despite the general—and probably justified—agreement on this matter, it is difficult to pinpoint al-Ghazālī's achievement here. There was undoubtedly tension between the ṣūfistic movement and official intellectuals; but at the same time several members of the official intellectual class were themselves ṣūfīs. Some of the attacks on ṣūfīs, too, when examined closely, are found to be due to the critic's belief that some of his quarry's *theological* doctrines were heretical. These are indications of the complexity of the matter; but that there was considerable tension cannot be doubted. Al-Ghazālī would have liked to expose himself to this tension in the same way as he had exposed himself to the tension with philosophy—by studying it in academic seclusion; but he came to realize that ṣūfism was existential, and that he could not attain to a full understanding of it without himself practising it as a way of life. So he made his courageous decision to abandon his professorship.

First, then, let us consider the influence on the ṣūfistic movement of what he did and wrote. The most distinctive feature of *The Revival of the Religious Sciences*, as has already been seen, is the insistence that the foundation of the ṣūfistic life is the observance of the outward forms of activity as prescribed in the scriptures and systematized in the "Islamic sciences". While we cannot suppose that a man like al-Qushayrī (d. 1072), who was both a jurist and a ṣūfī, was lax in his outward observances, it is probable that to him and many like him there did not seem to be much point in these observances; other ṣūfīs abandoned them altogether. For persons who felt doubts about the outward observances al-Ghazālī argues powerfully that they have some point, and he shows in detail what that point is. He thus made it clear that the ṣūfistic way of life was not an alternative to the formal Islamic observances but the complement or consummation of them, and that it therefore presupposed them. It seems legitimate to suppose that the expression of this attitude by al-Ghazālī would have various effects on the ṣūfistic movement. The antinomian sections would have to consider more seriously whether they were justified in neglecting the formal observances. Those who observed the forms without enthusiasm would come to a fuller insight into their importance. Those who hesitated to embrace the ṣūfistic way of life because they were conscious of the obligation of observing the standard forms would realize that the practice of ṣūfism, far from excluding the observance of the Sharīʿa, presupposed it. This last point, especially, ought to have led to a growth of the movement. At the same time it was more fully integrated into the life of Islamic society.

The twelfth century saw the first appearance of one of the most characteristic features of Islam as a religion, the dervish or mystical orders, and the question should be asked, how far al-Ghazālī is responsible for their appearance. These orders may be described as fraternities for spiritual training and discipline, and for the mutual support of the members, and to some extent resembled the monastic orders of Christendom. The first in time is usually reckoned to be the Qādiriyya, founded by ʿAbd-al-Qādir al-Jīlānī, who died in 1166. The movement for the founding of orders gained momentum through the centuries, and a modern list gives nearly two hundred orders, while many of these had several, partly independent, branch-orders.[3] At the beginning of the twentieth century large numbers of Muslims of the lower classes, though not full members of the orders, were attached to them, and found that what the austere Qur'ānic worship lacked was given to them in the *dhikr* of the order; the *dhikr* was a form of service or religious exercise, more sensuous than the formal prayers and more suited to stirring deep emotions, and perhaps attractive too in some cases because of the homely atmosphere of the small group. Now, if, as seems probable, al-Ghazālī contributed to the more rapid growth of the ṣūfistic movement and made it something within reach of the ordinary man, may he not be regarded as one of the chief causes of the appearance of the orders?

This question cannot be answered with a single word. The extent to which the worship of the orders was an alternative to the formal prayers rather than their complement has not been investigated; in practice it had sometimes become an alternative, and that is contrary to the direction in which al-Ghazālī had been moving. Again, the appearance of the orders was not a complete novelty. There had been previous experiments in spiritual discipline and a common life reaching back to before 800;[4] al-Ghazālī himself had established a monastic or semi-monastic institution at Ṭūs. What differentiated the orders was greater systematization and greater permanence. At most, then, al-Ghazālī can be credited with being one of the chief bearers of the spiritual movement out of which the orders came; but there is no evidence so far to justify assigning a special responsibility to him.

Next, al-Ghazālī's influence on the "Islamic sciences" and their bearers, the official intellectuals, must be considered. At first sight it might seem that this influence was small. The scholar-jurists continued to exist as a class, and there is no evidence of any widespread abandonment of worldliness. Ṣūfistic teaching was not included among the "Islamic sciences". No attention was paid to al-Ghazālī's speculations about a sphere of "immediate experience" above that of reason. In these respects he might seem to have failed. Nevertheless there is also something to say on the other side. His example must have inspired some intellectuals to be less worldly; from time to time genuine reforming zeal is met with. The non-ṣūfīs in the intellectual class became more tolerant of ṣūfism. Possibly for a time the teaching of the "Islamic sciences" became less academic. These are matters where first impressions are liable to be modified by later investigations, but provisionally they suggest that al-Ghazālī was not without influence on the intellectuals.

Finally, there is the question to what extent he influenced the life of the Islamic community as a whole. Although he produced no tidy theory and did not reform the official intellectual class, he seems to have had a wide influence. By largely removing the tension between ṣūfism and the "Islamic sciences" he brought the community much nearer to accepting a modified ideation suited to the situation in which it found itself. This modified ideation was implicit in his thinking rather than explicit. It was a new conception of the function of religion in the life of a society. Religion was no longer to be the guide of statesmen in their more far-reaching political decisions, as it had been in the earliest days, and as some religious intellectuals hoped it might be again.[5] It was instead to be the spiritual aspect of the life of the individual in his social relations. Al-Ghazālī seems to have assumed that not merely political decisions but all the outward forms of social life were beyond the ability of a man to control—this fixity of social forms was doubtless the result of the stabilization of the Traditions some two centuries before his time. Up to about 850 the religious aspirations of Muslims may be said to have been largely directed towards the Islamization of society. When this had been achieved in externals, there appeared as a new goal for religious aspirations the cultivation of greater beauty of character. Al-Ghazālī was not an innovator here, for many ordinary men were already looking in this direction, but he gave such men intellectual grounds for thinking their aspirations were sound.

Al-Ghazālī thought himself called to be the "renewer" of religion for the sixth Islamic century, and many, perhaps most, later Muslims have considered that he was indeed the "renewer" of this age. Some have even spoken of him as the greatest Muslim after Muḥammad. As his achievement is reviewed, it becomes clear that he was more of a prophet than a systematizer. Yet he is not simply a prophet, but is best described as a prophetic intellectual. He spoke to his fellows in terms of the highest thought of his time. Above all he made the individualistic aspect of religion intellectually respectable. It is probably his emphasis on the individualistic outlook that has appealed to the endemic individualism of Western scholars and gained him excessive praise; but he was far from being a sheer individualist. In his theorizing he sometimes fails to make explicit allowance for the communalism of the Sharīʻa, but he always presupposes it, and in his practice he effects a genuine integration of individualism and communalism. This is part of his title to greatness and of his achievement in "renewing" Islam.

In the background of the life of al-Ghazālī we see that much real piety continues to exist in the hearts of ordinary men despite the failure and corruption of their intellectual leaders. In his own life we see how the revivals or reforms, which frequently but unpredictably occur in the great religions, have their origin in the heart of a single man.

EXCURSUS

Ghazālī or *Ghazzālī*

THE spelling of the *nisba* of the great theologian has been for centuries a matter of dispute among scholars, and it is unlikely that we can now reach more than a probable conclusion on the matter. Yet it is worth while looking once again at the material.[1]

What may be called the standard view—Ibn Khallikān speaks of it as the *mash'hūr*—is that this *nisbá* is derived from *ghazzāl*, a spinner, or a vendor of spun yarn. In support of this derivation it is noted that the practice of deriving a *nisba* from a word of this form indicating an occupation is common in Jurjān and Khwarizm. A later writer like as-Subkī adds that the theologian's father was a spinner of wool, which he sold in his little shop.

The alternative view is that the correct spelling is Ghazālī and that it is derived from Ghazāla, a village near Ṭūs. This is found in the earliest source, as-Samʿānī, who died only half a century after the theologian. Unfortunately there appears to be no mention of the village except in discussions of the *nisba*. It is doubtless this fact that caused later scholars to be puzzled by the question. The lexicographically-minded Ibn-al-Athīr seems to have been the first to advocate the spelling Ghazzālī. The keenest interest in the question was in the middle of the fourteenth century. Al-Fayyūmī, who had made a special study of al-Ghazālī and compiled a lexicon of the less usual words in his writings, alleged that a descendant in the eighth generation (through the theologian's daughter) had told him that the family tradition was that the *nisba* was Ghazālī from the village. About the same time the polymath aṣ-Ṣafadī, besides quoting this point, said that the form Ghazālī was used by the theologian himself. As-Subkī (d. 1379) does not discuss the matter directly, but opposes these views by his allegation that the father of the theologian was a *ghazzāl*. The continuing problem of this *nisba* is shown by as-Sayyid al-Murtaḍā's mention of the possibility of its derivation from the feminine name Ghazāla.

Before setting out what I believe to be the most probable conclusion, there are some small points which may be cleared out of the way. Firstly, even if it is true that the theologian's father was a *ghazzāl*, that does not explain the *nisba*, since it was also attached to an earlier theologian, his uncle or grand-uncle;[2] the occupation may of course have been hereditary in the family. Secondly, the use of a *nisba* from an occupational name in Jurjān and Khwarizm is only slight support for such a practice at Ṭūs, which is not in either of these regions, though comparatively near them. Thirdly, the absence of mention of a village Ghazāla is not in itself conclusive, since it may have been small and unimportant, or may have disappeared; there is no mention in Yāqūt's *Mu-ʿjam al-Buldān* of a village of Khuwār in the Ṭabarān section of Ṭūs, from which one of al-Ghazālī's teachers came, though several villages of this name are mentioned.[3] Fourthly, the motive (mentioned by Brockelmann)[4] of avoiding a name suggesting low origin is only one of several possible motives; scholars with a predilection for asceticism might prefer the form which indicated the poverty of this great theologian-mystic's home.[5] Moreover, it is unlikely that the theologian himself, especially after his departure from Baghdad and adoption of a measure of voluntary poverty, would be ashamed of his origin; while, since he had only daughters, his descendants did not bear the name. Fifthly, the existence of Persian poets or other persons who have or use the form Ghazzālī does not make it certain that this is how the theologian spelt it.[6]

With these small points disposed of, the way is open to assert that Ghazālī is the more likely form. This assertion is based on an analogy with the principle of *difficilior lectio potius*. When the derivation from *ghazzāl* is so obvious, why should another have been put forward? Motives can, indeed, be suggested, but they are all far from certain. On the other hand, if we suppose that the original form was Ghazālī, as the oldest source states, it is understandable that scholars, finding this obscure and unlikely, would emend it to Ghazzālī. The acceptance of the form Ghazālī as the more probable does not necessitate acceptance of the derivation from a village of Ghazāla (still less from a woman); this may be merely the baseless conjecture of as-Samʿānī; at the same time our information is so meagre that the existence of a village of this name cannot be ruled out as impossible. The conclusion therefore is that, while much inevitably remains obscure, there is a preponderance of probability in favour of Ghazālī.

NOTES, CHRONOLOGICAL TABLE AND BIBLIOGRAPHY

N

NOTES

I

1. London, 1961; referred to in the notes as *Integration.*

2. The complexity of the intelligentsia is brought out in F. Znaniecki, *The Social Rôle of the Men of Knowledge*, 1940.

II

1. Cf. *Integration*; also "The Conception of the Charismatic Community in Islam", *Numen*, vii. 77-90.

2. Cf. E. G. Browne, *Literary History of Persia*, Cambridge, 1928, i. 365 f.

3. Miskawayh in H. F. Amedroz and D. S. Margoliouth, *The Eclipse of the ʿAbbasid Caliphate*, Oxford, 1921, i. 352 (iv. 396).

4. Cf. B. Spüler, *Iran in früh-islamischer Zeit*, Wiesbaden, 1952, 129.

5. Cf. *Muhammad at Mecca*, Oxford, 1953; also the opening chapters of *Integration.*

6. Cf. *Integration*, 102.

7. Cf. N. Daniel, *Islam and the West: the Making of an Image*, Edinburgh, 1960.

8. See ch. VI below.

9. But the identification of Persians with Shīʿite doctrines in the early period must not be exaggerated; the identification has only been close since the sixteenth century.

10. Browne, *Literary History of Persia*, ii. 129-41.

10a. He is said to have written some books in Persian, such as *Kīmiyā' as-Saʿāda*, and appears to have written letters in Persian (*Faḍā'il al-Ānām*). In *Maqṣad*, 73, he uses the form Kurkānī (Gurgānī) for Jurjānī, although the scholar Yāqūt (*Muʿjam al-Buldān*, s.v.) says the K form is never used in Arabic.

11. Some authorities say it ought to be Ghazzālī, the descendant of the *ghazzāl* or spinner, but this is less likely. Cf. 183 below.

12. *Iljām*; cf. p. 148 below.

13. A. Mez, *The Renaissance of Islam* (Eng. tr.), Patna, 1937, 182.

14. I have not been able to find the source of this date 470/1077, given, presumably independently, by Bouyges and M. Smith.

15. Mez, 191.

16. Cf. J. Pedersen, art. "Madrasa", IV, in *EI(S)*. Also Subk. iii. 135-45, esp. 137. He may have been imitating the seminaries of the sectarian Karrāmites and Qarmaṭians (cf. Massignon, *Passion*, i. 166); and his aim was doubtless to counter sectarian views; cf. p. 106 below.

17. We do not know where the camp was; it presumably moved. During this period he may have travelled to Zūzan in Afghanistan; he is said to have studied under a traditionist there (cf. SM, i. 19 f.; Subk. iv. 114).

III

1. The best general survey is that of Richard Walzer, "Islamic Philosophy", in S. Radhakrishnan, *History of Philosophy, Eastern and Western*, London, 1953, ii. 120-48. Older accounts, partly out of date, are: T. J. de Boer, *The History of Philosophy in Islam*, London, 1903; De Lacy O'Leary, *Arabic Thought and its Place in History*, London, 1929. A useful bibliographical introduction is: P. J. de Menasce, *Arabische Philosophie* (Bibliographische Einführungen in das Studium der Philosophie, 6), Bern, 1948. For the Christian translators into Arabic an excellent compendium of information is: G. Graf, *Geschichte der christlichen arabischen Literatur*, vol. ii (Vatican City, 1947), under individual names. Further information will be found in Montgomery Watt, *Islamic Philosophy and Theology*, Edinburgh, 1962, chs. 5, 10, 15. Cf. also R. Walzer, "New Light on the Arabic translations of Aristotle", *Oriens*, vi. (1953), 91-142.

2. Graf, ii. 109-11.

3. Max Meyerhof, "Von Alexandrien nach Bagdad; ein Beitrag zur Geschichte des philosophischen und medizinischen Unterrichts bei den Arabern", *Sitzungsberichte der preussischen Akademie der Wissenschaften*, 1930, Philosophisch-historische Klasse, 389-429.

4. P. Kraus, "Zu Ibn al-Muqaffaʿ", *Rivista degli Studi Orientali*, xiv (1933-1934), 1-20.

5. Full name: Abū-Yūsuf Yaʿqūb ibn-Is'ḥāq of the Arab tribe of Kinda. The sources for his life are examined by Muḥammad ʿAbd-al-Hādī Abū-Rīda, *Al-Kindī wa-Falsafatu-hu*, also printed as introduction to *Rasā'il al-Kindī al-Falsafiyya* (both Cairo, 1950/1369). The chief Arabic biographical sources and modern treatments are listed under the name of each author in *GAL* and *GALS*. There are notices of the chief writers in the *Encyclopaedia of Islam*, second edition in progress. Most of the philosophers in the following list are treated in Meyerhof, "Von Alexandrien . . .", 413-27.

6. Cf. Ibn-an-Nadīm, *Fihrist*; also al-Masʿūdī, *Murūj adh-Dhahab*, Paris, 1861, viii. 179 f.; Yāqūt, *Irshād al-ʿArīb*, i. 158 f.

7. The Arabic sources are summarized in Muṣṭafā ʿAbd-ar-Razzāq Pāshā, *Faylasūf al-ʿArab wa-l-Muʿallim ath-Thānī* (Cairo, 1945/1364).

8. For the biography see A. J. Arberry, "Avicenna: His Life and Times", in G. M. Wickens (ed.), *Avicenna: Scientist and Philosopher*, London, 1952, 9-28.

9. J. Schacht and M. Meyerhof, *The Medico-Philosophical Controversy between Ibn Buṭlan of Baghdad and Ibn Riḍwan of Cairo*, Cairo, 1937. A brief notice of this is given by Schacht in *ZDMG*, 90 (1936), 526-45.

10. Cf. *Integration*, 120-3; also H. A. R. Gibb, "The Social Significance of the Shuʿūbīya", *Studia Orientali Ioanni Pedersen . . . dicata*, Copenhagen, 1953, 105-14. Niẓām-al-Mulk makes Maḥmūd of Ghazna say that "most of the scribes of ʿIraq belonged to heretical sects and would wreck Turkish interests" (*Book of Government*, 69).

11. Walzer, "Islamic Philosophy", 127-30, emphasizes that the primary contact of the Arabs was with later Greek philosophy, which is still imperfectly known.

12. P. Kraus, *Abi Bakr . . . Raghensis Opera Philosophica*, Cairo, 1939, i. 27; A. J. Arberry, *The Spiritual Physick of Rhazes*, London, 1950, 29.

13. Kraus, 18, freely translated; cf. Arberry, 20.

14. Kraus, 29; Arberry, 31.

15. Kraus, 108; Arberry, 14.

16. *Rasā'il al-Kindī al-Falsafiyya*, 272-80.

17. *Risāla fī-l-ʿAql*, ed. M. Bouyges, Beirut, 1938.

18. *Rasā'il al-Kindī*, 182-4.

19. *Ibid.* 104; 244-61.

20. *Ibid.* 278.

21. Cf. H. Frankfort, *Kingship and the Gods*, Chicago, 1948.

22. *K. as-Siyāsāt al-Madaniyya*, Hyderabad (1927)/1346, 53.

23. For some support of the view that al-Fārābī was not a Shīʿite cf. F. M. Najjār, "Fārābī's Political Philosophy and Shīʿism" (*Studia Islamica*, xiv. 57-72). For the Shīʿite conception of the leader see *Integration*, 104-10.

24. *K. al-Madīna al-Fāḍila*, ed. Fr. Dieterici, Leiden, 1895, 58 f.; cf. *Siyāsāt*, 49 f. To be consistent with other parts of this study, *ʿaql* has been translated "reason", though in this context "intellect" would be more suitable; a discussion of the exact meaning of the various terms is beyond our present scope, but a lucid exposition of the matter will be found in F(azlur-) Rahman, *Prophecy in Islam*, London, 1958, ch. 1. For the word translated "prudent", *mutaʿaqqil*, cf. *Risāla fī-'l-ʿAql*, 7. 5 and *Fuṣūl al-Madanī*, p. 84.

25. *Al-Madīna al-Fāḍila*, 60 f. Cf. also *Fuṣūl al-Madanī*, ed. D. M. Dunlop, Cambridge, 1961, § 54; the fresh problems raised by this work have not yet been adequately treated.

26. *K. as-Siyāsāt*, 55 f., translated by Fazlur-Rahman, *Prophecy*, 40 f.

27. *K. an-Najāt*, Cairo, 1938/1357, 167 f., tr. by Fazlur-Rahman, *Avicenna's Psychology*, Oxford, 1952, 36 f. Cf. *K. ash-Shifā'* ("Avicenna's De Anima"), ed. Fazlur-Rahman, London, 1959, 248-50; and index.

28. *K. an-Najāt*, 304-6. Cf. Louis Gardet, *La Pensée religieuse d'Avicenne*, Paris, 1951, 125-8; Fazlur-Rahman, *Prophecy*, 30-64, gives a useful exposition, but does not distinguish the views of al-Fārābī and Avicenna. Fazlur-Rahman has done excellent work in tracing the Hellenistic sources of Islamic philosophy, and it is unfortunate that he has mistakenly attacked Gardet at one or two points and failed to realize that their work is complementary and not contradictory. Besides asking about the source

of a view we must also ask about the motive for adopting it and its relation to the contemporary historical situation. Al-Ghazālī, summarizing the views of the philosophers in *Maqāṣid*, 319 f., is close to Avicenna, and mentions the scholar-jurists as mediating between the prophet and the ordinary people.

29. *K. al-Ishārāt wa-t-Tanbīhāt* ("Livre des théorèmes et des avertissements"), ed. J. Forget, Leiden, 1892, 198-207; French tr. by A. M. Goichon ("Livre des directives et remarques"), Paris and Beirut, 1951, 483-501.

30. Abū-Shujā' ar-Rūdhrāwarī, *Dhayl Kitāb Tajārib al-Umam*, in Amedroz and Margoliouth, *Eclipse of the 'Abbasid Caliphate*, iii. 76 f. (tr. vi. 77 f.).

31. *Munqidh*, English translation in *Faith and Practice*.

32. The passage quoted in SM, i. 9 (and translated by M. Smith, *Al-Ghazālī*, 14 f.) implies that he went to a ṣūfī teacher in Ṭūs before 1077. On the other hand, there is nothing to suggest that familiarity with the sceptical arguments of the Bāṭinites had anything to do with his scepticism.

33. *Tahdhīb al-Akhlāq*, Cairo, 1911/1329, 11.

34. In the allegory of the cave in the *Republic*, ordinary men argue about mere shadows.

35. The argument received much attention from theologians in the century before al-Ghazālī, and had been developed with greater subtlety than the above summary suggests. Cf. al-Bāqillānī (d. 1013), *K. al-Bayān* ("Miracle and Magic: a treatise on the nature of the apologetic miracle and its differentiation from charisms, trickery, divination, magic and spells"), ed. R. J. McCarthy, Beirut, 1958.

36. *Maqāṣid*, 3.

37. *Tahāfut*, 352 ff. and frequently.

38. *Maqāṣid*, 320.

39. *Najāt*, 168; cf. *Avicenna's Psychology*, 37.

40. *Tahāfut*, 177.

41. Goldziher has collected many instances of this attitude scattered over several centuries (see "Stellung" in Bibliography).

42. *Faith and Practice*, 55 (126).

43. Bouyges, *Chronologie*, 2; he attended a special course of lectures in June 1093 and was present when the oath was taken to

the new caliph al-Mustaẓ'hir in Feb. 1094 (from Ibn-al-Athīr, etc.).

44. *Faith and Practice*, 30 (85).

45. *Tahāfut al-Falāsifa.*

46. Bouyges, *Chronologie*, 23.

47. *Tahāfut*, 180. 5; cf. 339.

48. *Ibid.* (sections) 4, 5, 9, 10, 11, 12, 18.

49. *Ibid.* p. 13.

50. In *The Golden Mean in Belief*, *ad init.*, al-Ghazālī says reason and revelation are complementary; reason is like human sight and revelation like the sun. This was probably written soon after *The Inconsistency of the Philosophers*, and may be the proposed work on *The Foundations of Belief* (*Qawā'id al-ʿAqā'id*) mentioned there (p. 78).

51. *Tahāfut*, 376; cf. *Faith and Practice*, 37 f.

52. §§ 1, 2, 14, 15, 16, 17, 3.

53. *Tahāfut*, 96.

54. §§ 13, 6, 7, 8.

54a. Cf. the remarks of R. D. Laing in *The Divided Self* (London, 1960) on "the ontologically insecure person" (p. 67) and "temporary states of dissociation of the self from the body" (p. 82).

55. *Tahāfut*, 376.

56. Al-Juwaynī (Subk. iii. 270; iv. 103. 15); Ibn-Ḥazm (d. 1064), Goldziher, "Stellung", 27.

57. It is exaggerated by Jabre, *Certitude*, 291-3, 316 f., 371; cf. Watt, "Study", 129.

58. Cf. *Miʿyār*, 37 f., where he points out how the (philosophers') logical definition of "universal" (*kullī*) gives a superior solution of a point of legal interpretation. In *Maqāṣid*, 43, he shows an awareness of the logical weaknesses of the theologians.

59. *Faith and Practice*, 32-43 (90-107).

60. *Miʿyār*, *ad fin.* (195), promises *Mīzān al-ʿAmal.*

61. Cf. *JRAS*, 1952, 38-40, 45.

62. Bouyges, *Chronologie*, 29, n. 6. Al-Ghazālī's virtual rejection of *The Criterion of Action* may explain the state of the text; if he did not authorize its "publication" (by copying), the single manuscript may have come into the hands of an unscrupulous person, who put it in its present form.

63. *Miʿyār*, 21-3.

64. *Qisṭās*, 162.

65. Goldziher, "Stellung", § 2, pp. 16-19.

66. Cf. edition and French translation by V. Chelhot (see Bouyges, *Chronologie*, 57n.).

IV

1. *Book of Government*, 244; cf. Goldziher, *Streitschrift*, 38, 44, etc.

2. Cf. *Streitschrift*, 40 f.; Browne, *Literary History of Persia*, ii. 206; M. G. S. Hodgson, art. "Bāṭiniyya" in *EI*[2].

3. *Integration*, 104-10; "Shīʿism".

4. B. Lewis, *The Origins of Ismāʿīlism*, Cambridge, 1940, 76-89.

5. Cf. *GAL*, i. 236-8; *GALS*, i. 379-81; Adel Awa, *L'Esprit critique des "Frères de la Pureté"*, Beirut, 1948; I. R. al-Fārūqī, "On the Ethics of the Brethren of Purity", *Muslim World*, 50 (1960), 109-21, 193-8, 252-8.

6. Lewis, *Origins*, 92 f.; Goldziher, *Streitschrift*, 23.

7. *Streitschrift*, 42 f.; cf. Jabre, *Certitude*, 316 f.

8. *EI*[2], art. "al-Bāsasīrī".

9. Goldziher, *Streitschrift*, 12 f.; ash-Shahrastānī, *K. al-Milal*, Cairo, 1948/1368, i. 339-45 (= Cureton, 150-2).

10. *Integration*, 67-78.

11. W. Ivanow, *A Creed of the Fatimids*, Bombay, 1936, 47-50; for its soundness as an exposition of earlier views cf. p. vi.

12. In *Al-Majālis al-Mustanṣiriyya* (ed. Muḥammad Kāmil Ḥusayn, Cairo, n.d.), 29 f., the Qur'ān and the imam are spoken of as "equal partners" (*qarīnān*). (Cf. *Islamic Research Association Miscellany*, i. 146.) This book, probably composed about 1062, also speaks of the obligation to retain the *ẓāhir* along with the *bāṭin* (p. 19, etc.)—a doctrine which limits the control of ideation by the imam, but which was rejected by the Assassins and other revolutionaries. Such a doctrine was more appropriate for men charged (like the Fāṭimids) with the responsibility of keeping order in a mixed community. For the more conservative outlook of the Fāṭimids cf. B. Lewis, *Origins*, 85 f., and H. F. Hamdani in *JRAS*, 1933, 365.

13. J. Sauvaget, *Alep* (Paris, 1941), gives an idea of what the period of anarchy meant in one locality.

13a. Cf. A. J. Toynbee, *A Study of History*, vii. 415.

14. *Iqtiṣād*, 106; *Book of Government*, 63; cf. p. 100 below.

15. Bouyges, *Chronologie*, 31.

16. Apparently *Qawāṣim al-Bāṭiniyya* (Bouyges, 85).

17. Jabre, "Biographie", esp. 91-4; also *Certitude*; cf. Watt, "Study", 129; and p. 142 below.

18. *Faith and Practice*, 56 (127).

19. *Iqtiṣād*, 104-8 (part 4, ch. 3).

V

1. Cf. "Khārijite Thought under the Umayyads", *Der Islam*, xxxvi (1961), 215-31; and *Integration*, 214-18.

2. Cf. "Shīʿism"; also *Integration*, 104-10, 220 f.

3. Cf. "Political Attitudes".

4. Cf. J. Schacht, *The Origins of Muhammadan Jurisprudence*, Oxford, 1950: *Integration*, 191-4, 272.

5. Cf. *Integration*, 277-9, 122; and p. 18 above.

6. Cf. *Integration*, 260, 264, etc., § 2.

7. Cf. *Integration*, 169, etc.

8. Al-Masʿūdī, *Murūj*, ii. 162; Niẓām-al-Mulk, *Book of Government*, 63; *ID*, i. 15 top; *Iqtiṣād*, 106; cf. Goldziher in *ZDMG*, lxii. 2 n.; also p. 82 above.

9. *Integration*, 120; cf. Massignon, *Passion*, i. 189, 195, with references to aṭ-Ṭabarī, *Annales*, iii. 517, 519-22.

10. Cf. "Political Attitudes".

11. E.g. Ghaylān, executed 743 (Montgomery Watt, *Free Will and Predestination*, London, 1948, 40-8). Cf. A. S. Tritton, *Muslim Theology*, London, 1948, 23-7, 54 f.

12. Goldziher, "Beiträge zur . . . ḥanbalitischen Bewegungen", *ZDMG*, lxii, esp. 5-7.

13. *Ibid.* 1-4.

14. *Passion*, esp. 161-82, 197-220.

15. *Ibid.* 161-82; cf. *GALS*, i. 249 f. (the date of his death should be corrected to 297/910).

16. *Passion*, 151-9; cf. 349 f.

17. Cf. Cl. Cahen, art. "Buwayhids", in *EI*².

18. The best available study is in H. Laoust's "Introduction" to *La Profession de foi d'Ibn Baṭṭa* (Damascus, 1958).

19. Subk. iii. 53 f.; cf. Goldziher in *ZDMG*, lxii. 13. Maḥmūd favoured the Karrāmite form of Sunnism—Laoust, *Profession*, xcii. n., etc.

20. Ibn-Rajab, *Adh-Dhayl ʿalā Ṭabaqāt al-Ḥanābila*, Cairo, 1953/1372, 52; also ed. H. Laoust and S. Dahan, Damascus, 1951, 66.

21. Ibn-al-Athīr, *sub anno* 456; cf. E. G. Browne, *Literary History of Persia*, ii. 171-4. The exact strength of the Ḥanbalites is difficult to estimate. Al-Ghazālī (*ID*, i. 25—book 1, ch. 2, *ad fin.*) says they are fewer in number than Shāfiʿites, Ḥanafites and Mālikites. If this judgement is correct, either the impression given by the Ḥanbalite sources exaggerates their importance, or they were more important in Baghdad than elsewhere.

22. *GALS*, i. 562, cf. *ZDMG*, lxii. 9.

23. Laoust, *Profession*, cvi; Ibn-Rajab, *Dhayl*, 19 (24).

24. Goldziher, *ZDMG*, lxii. 17-21; Massignon, *Passion*, 366 f.; George Makdisi, "Autograph Diary of an Eleventh-century Historian of Baghdad", *BSOAS*, xviii (1956), 9-31, 239-60; xix (1957), 13-48, 281-303, 426-43; *id.* "Nouveaux Détails sur l'affaire d'Ibn ʿAqīl", *Mélanges Louis Massignon*, Damascus, 1957, iii. 91-126; Laoust, *loc. cit.*

25. *ZDMG*, lxii. 9 f.; Laoust, cviii; Subk. iii. 98 f., iv. 251; Ibn-al-Athīr, viii. 124 (year 470, not 485, as in *ZDMG*).

26. *ID*, i. 51-72; *Vivification*, § 13 f.

27. *ID*, i. 55; Hujwīrī, 98-100; as-Sulamī, *Ṭabaqāt aṣ-Ṣūfiyya*, ed. J. Pedersen, Leiden, 1960, 10. 8.

28. *ID*, i. 53.

29. *ID*, i. 57 f.

30. *K. ar-Riʿāya*, ed. Margaret Smith, London, 1940, 84-133; *Qūt al-Qulūb*, Cairo, 1932/1357, ii. 8-17 (§ 31). Niẓām-al-Mulk, *Book of Government*, 78-90, has stories of leading judges who were dishonest; even if not true these stories show the low reputation of the class.

31. *ID*, i. 2 f.; SM, i. 57-9.

32. *ID*, i. 53; SM. i. 358 quotes a similar saying from the *Ḥilya*

of Abū-Nuʿaym, and a report that Sufyān ibn-ʿUyayna attributed a saying about salt to ʿĪsā.

33. *ID*, i. 59-61; for the use of *fatwās* cf. Massignon, *Passion*, i. 220 f.

34. *ID*, i. 49.

35. Quotations in *Iqtiṣād* from *Tahāfut* (49), *Mustaẓʾhirī* (107), *Miḥakk* (9), *Miʿyār* (9); cf. Bouyges, *Chronologie*, 34.

36. *Faith and Practice*, 27-9.

37. *ID*, i. 18 f.

38. *Iqtiṣād*, *ad fin*.

39. *Arbaʿīn*, 24.

40. *Iqtiṣād*, 6-8, second *tamhīd*; cf. *Arbaʿīn*, 23-5. The point here made is also made by Jabre, *Certitude*, 171, and by C. A. Nallino, *Oriente Moderno*, xv (1935), 59. Cf. also p. 148 below.

41. *Irshād*, see Bibliography.

42. *Al-ʿAqīda an-Niẓāmiyya*, Cairo, 1948/1367. There is a not altogether satisfactory German translation by H. Klopfer, Cairo (1958).

43. For the date of Abū-Bakr ibn-al-ʿArabī's first visit to Baghdad cf. Ibn-al-ʿImād, *Shadharāt adh-Dhahab*, iv. 141 f. It is less likely that al-Ghazālī lectured on this work on Abū-Bakr's second visit in May/June 1097 (cf. Abū-Bakr's statement in *ʿAwāṣim al-Qawāṣim*, quoted by Jabre, "Biographie", 87—but the date is not "February"). For the use of texts in lecturing cf. Mez, *Renaissance of Islam*, 179 f.; also A. S. Tritton, *Materials on Muslim Education in the Middle Ages*, London, 1957.

44. Subk. iv. 103. 15.

45. E.g. al-Juwaynī's *Irshād*; cf. L. Gardet and M. M. Anawati; *Introduction à la théologie musulmane*, Paris, 1948, 153-69.

46. *Iqtiṣād*, 13-15; *Irshād*, 15/35–17/37.

47. *Irshād*, 25/49–28/56; *Iqtiṣād*, 20 f.

48. An interesting philosophical argument is the second argument for the visibility of God, *Iqtiṣād*, 32-4 (cf. *ʿAqīda Niẓāmiyya*, 28, not understood by Klopfer). The close parallelism to *Maʿārij al-Quds* (Cairo, 1927/1346), 180-2, raises problems, since the *Maʿārij* is Neoplatonic and cannot be authentic unless like the *Maqāṣid* it is an objective statement of the philosophers' views.

VI

1. *Faith and Practice*, 57 (128).

2. The fullest treatment of the early ṣūfī movement is in Louis Massignon's *Essai* (see Bibliography), chs. 4 and 5. A reliable short work in English is *Sufism: an Account of the Mystics of Islam*, by A. J. Arberry, London, 1950.

3. *Essai*, 153-6.

4. The main point here is made, for example, in *Mystical Elements in Mohammed*, by John Clark Archer (New Haven, 1924), a book which, though now out-dated in part, has some useful suggestions.

5. Massignon, *Essai*, 174-201, 236 f.

6. *Essai*, 316, etc. Cf. also p. 103 above.

7. *Ibid.* 314.

8. *Ibid.* 273-86, esp. 276; R. C. Zaehner's insistence on Indian influence, though probably correct, does not affect the wider questions (*Hindu and Muslim Mysticism*, London, 1960, 86-109).

9. *Essai*, 315.

10. Cf. Arberry, *Sufism*, 31; Massignon, *Essai*, 159 f. (protests made against the wealth of the Umayyads).

11. *Essai*, 189 (al-Ḥasan), 249 f. (al-Muḥāsibī).

12. It must be admitted, however, that the break between mysticism and worldliness was far from complete; Ibn-Abī-Dunyā (d. 894), reckoned a ṣūfī, was also tutor to the heir to the caliphate (Massignon, *Essai*, 232, 240).

13. Cf. p. 108ff. above.

14. Subk. iv. 102.

15. SM, i. 9; cf. Macdonald, "Life", 90; M. Smith, 14 f.

16. Subk. iv. 9 f. Abū-ʿAlī al-Faḍl ibn-Muḥammad (*Ibid.* 126. 14 Abū-ʿAlī al-ʿAlā'ī is presumably the same); cf. Hujwīrī, 169. Al-Ghazālī quotes from him, *Maqṣad*, 73.

17. Ibn-al-Athīr, year 485, notice of Niẓām-al-Mulk.

18. Yāqūt, *Muʿjam al-Buldān*, ii. 730, 18.

19. Cf. *Mīzān*, 44, and *ID*, iii. 17—discussed in Watt, "Authenticity", *JRAS*, 1952, 39 f.

20. *Faith and Practice*, 55 (126).

21. *Ibid.* 54-8 (122-8).

22. *Murūj*, viii. 188 f.

23. "Life", 98; also his art. "al-Ghazzālī" in *EI*[1].

24. "Biographie", esp. 91-4; cf. also his *Certitude* and *La Notion de la Maʿrifa chez Ghazali*, Beirut, 1958.

25. "Biographie", 89, 102.

26. *Ibid.* 90 f.

27. *Ibid.* 90, quoting Subk. iv. 109. Just above Jabre has apparently assimilated fear of death and fear of Judgement to one another; but they are very different.

28. Cf. "Study", 123; also Bouyges, *Chronologie*, 32.

29. *Faith and Practice*, 86-152, esp. 90-130.

30. *Ibid.* 59 f. (130 f.).

31. Ibn-al-Athīr, *sub anno* 488.

32. Jabre, "Biographie", 87; cf. p. 120 n. 43 above.

33. Bouyges, *Chronologie*, 4 n. 1, quoting Ibn-al-Athīr, *sub anno* 492.

34. Cf. Bouyges, *ibid.* n. 5, and 45 f.

35. *Ibid.* 4 n. 7.

36. *Faith and Practice*, 75 f. (152 f.).

37. Bouyges, 73, quoting Ibn-Khallikān, i. 587.

38. Bouyges, 4 n. 7, last name; Subk. iv. 65; he was born in 1093/4.

39. Bouyges, 81; G. F. Hourani, *Journal of the American Oriental Society*, lxxix [1959], 233.

40. Subk. iv. 106.

41. *Iljām*, 4, slightly abbreviated.

42. Cf. H. Laoust, *Essai sur Ibn Taimīya*, Cairo, 1939, 481.

43. *Mishkāt*, 35 (77); Laoust, *op. cit.* 155 n., says this *via media* is also found in the *Iqtiṣād*, but gives no reference.

44. Cf. p. 67 above.

45. Cf. p. 119 n. 40 above.

46. The non-Arabist, or the Arabist in a hurry, may obtain a good idea of the scope of the work from G. H. Bousquet's French "analysis" (see Bibliography under *Vivification*). Some of the more elementary parts are expounded briefly in *The Beginning of Guidance*, in *Faith and Practice*, 86-152.

VII

1. Cf. *Integration*, chs. 2 and 3.
2. Cf. p. 81f. above.
3. Cf. p. 102 above.
4. *Faith and Practice*, 62 (135); cf. *Mishkāt*, 33 (74), 39 (81) ff. The choice of term is probably due to Greek influence; cf. *Averroes' Tahafut al-Tahafut*, tr. S. Van den Berg, London, 1954, ii, 11 foot. Since stating in *JRAS*, 1952, 27, that this technical use of *dhawq* was not found in the *ID* (*Iḥyā'*), I have discovered or had pointed out to me several instances. But I am still of the opinion that in certain parts of the *ID* (which are therefore perhaps "early") al-Ghazālī had not adopted the conception; cf. "Study", 126.
5. *ID*, iv. 354; cf. *JRAS*, 1952, 27.
6. *Arbaʿīn*, 57; cf. 23. The relation of the last ten sections of this work to the books of the *Revival* is: 31; 33; 34; 32a; 32b; 37; 35b; 36a; 36b; 40. Thus books 35a, 38, 39 are omitted.
7. Hujwīrī, 341; cf. *K. al-Lumaʿ*, Cairo, 1960/1380, 195.
8. Cf. Hujwīrī, 229.
9. *Faith and Practice*, 55 (125).
10. Hujwīrī 69; cf. 48 f., 53.

VIII

1. E.g. Ibn-Taymiyya, *Radd ʿalā 'l-Manṭiqiyyīn*.
2. Cf. Gardet and Anawati, *Introduction à la théologie musulmane*, 76, "le conservatisme figé".
3. Louis Massignon, art. "Tarīḳa" in *EI(S)*.
4. Massignon, *Essai*, 156 f.
5. Aspirations for a restoration of a caliphate (with power) adhering to the principles of the Sharīʿa are probably behind al-Māwardī's (d. 1058) *Institutions of Government* (*Al-Aḥkām as-Sulṭāniyya*); cf H. A. R. Gibb in *Islamic Culture*, xi (1937), 291-302. To al-Ghazālī is ascribed, probably correctly, a work on government in the Persian tradition (and in Persian), *Naṣīhat al-Mulūk*; cf. Fr. Meier in *ZDMG*. 93 (1939), 395-408. This suggests he had abandoned the attempt to assert the Sharīʿa in the conduct of

government. (An English translation by F. R. C. Bagley is in course of publication.)

Excursus

1. Supporters of "z": as-Samʿānī (d. 1167) as quoted by Ibn-Khallikān but denied by SM; aṣ-Ṣafadī (d. 1363), *Wāfī*, i. 277. 15; al-Fayyūmī (d. 1368), *Al-Miṣbāḥ al-Munīr*, s.v. GH.Z.L. Supporters of "zz": Ibn-al-Athīr (d. 1234), *Lubāb*, ii. s.v. (prefers "zz" but says "z" also held); Ibn-Khallikān (d. 1282), s.v. "Aḥmad al-Ghazālī" ("zz" normal, but other is possible). Ibn aṭ-Ṭiqṭaqā, (fl. 1301), *al-Fakhrī*, ed. Derenbourg, 206; Ibn-al-ʿImād (d. 1679), *Shadharāt adh-Dhahab*, iv. 11; SM (d. 1791), i. 18 f. gives views of a number of writers, mainly in favour of "zz". D. B. Macdonald, after a full discussion of the evidence (*JRAS*, 1902, 18-22), leaves the question undecided. C. Brockelmann (*GALS*, i. 744 n.) prefers "zz". Cf. C. A. Nallino in *Oriente Moderno*, xv (1935). 58 f.

2. Subk. iii. 35 f. Such chronological indications as are gained from the notice suggest that grand-uncle is more likely; but D. B. Macdonald's support for this matter ("Life", 74 n. 2) is based on an inferior text.

3. SM, i. 19 f.; he may be mentioned by Yāqūt in *Muʿjam al-Buldān*, iii. 10, as ʿAbd-Allāh b. Muḥammad al-Khuwārī.

4. *GALS*, i. 744 n.

5. Cf. the exaggerations of the poverty of some of Muḥammad's Companions, *EI*², art. "Ahl al-Ṣuffa".

6. *GALS*, *loc. cit.*; cf. SM, i. 19. 9-14, three other scholars.

CHRONOLOGICAL TABLE

A.D. 1058	Birth of al-Ghazālī at Tūs (450 A.H.)
c. 1069	Began studies at Ṭūs
c. 1073	Went to Gurgan to study
1074–1077	Study at Ṭūs
c. 1077	Went to Nishapur to study
1084	Death of al-Fārmadhī
1085, Aug.	Death of al-Juwaynī, left Nishapur (iv. 478)
1091, July	Arrival in Baghdad (v. 484)
1092, Oct. 14	Niẓām-al-Mulk killed (10. ix. 485)
1091 (late)–1094	Study of philosophy
1093, June	Present at sermons in Niẓāmiyya
1094, Feb.	Present at oath to new caliph, al-Mustaẓ'hir
1094	Finished *Maqāṣid*
1095, Jan. 12	Finished *Tahāfut*
1095, Feb.	Tutush killed, Barkiyāruq recognized in Baghdad
1095, July	Impediment in speech (vii. 488)
1095, Nov.	Left Baghdad (xi. 488)
1096, Nov.–Dec.	Made pilgrimage of 489
1097, June	Abū-Bakr ibn-al-ʿArabī saw him in Baghdad (vi. 490)
c. 1099	Went by Ḥamadhān to Tūs
1104, Dec.	Barkiyāruq died
1106, July	Returned to teaching in Nishapur (xi. 499)
c. 1108	Wrote *Deliverance from Error*
1109, Aug. 5	Finished *Mustaṣfā* (on law) (6. i. 503)
c. 1110	Returned to Ṭūs
1111, Dec.	Finished *Iljām*
1111, Dec. 18	Death (14. vi. 505)

BIBLIOGRAPHY

(This bibliography contains the works most frequently referred to, and the abbreviations used. Other bibliographical details are found in the footnotes, and are indicated in the index by an asterisk.)

Bouyges (Maurice), *Chronologie* = *Essai de chronologie des œuvres de al-Ghazali*, ed. and brought up to date by M. Allard, Beirut, 1959.

BSOAS = *Bulletin of the School of Oriental and African Studies* (London).

EI[1] = *Encyclopedia of Islam*, first edition, Leiden, 1913–1942.

EI[2] = *Encyclopedia of Islam*, second edition, vol. i, 1960.

EI(S) = *EI*[1] as revised in *A Shorter Encyclopedia of Islam* or *Handwörterbuch des Islam*.

Faith and Practice: see al-Ghazālī.

GAL = Carl Brockelmann, *Geschichte der arabischen Literatur*, second edition, Leiden, 1943–1949.

GALS = Carl Brockelmann, *Geschichte der arabischen Literatur*, first edition, Supplementbände, Leiden, 1937–1942.

Al-Ghazālī: *Arbaʿīn* = *K. al-Arbaʿīn*, Cairo (1925)/1344. ("The Book of the Forty.")

Faith and Practice = *The Faith and Practice of al-Ghazālī*, London, 1953; translations of the *Munqidh* and *Bidāyat al-Hidāya* by W. Montgomery Watt; a number in brackets gives the page of the Arabic text used.

Fayṣal = *Fayṣal at-Tafriqa bayn al-Islam wa-'z-Zandaqa*, in *Al-Jawāhir al-Ghawālī*, Cairo, 1934/1353. ("The Decisive Criterion for distinguishing between Islam and Unbelief.")

ID = *Iḥyā' ʿUlūm ad-Dīn*, Cairo (1898)/1316. ("The Revival of the Religious Sciences"); see also *Vivification*.

Iljām = *Iljām al-ʿAwāmm ʿan ʿIlm al-Kalām*, Cairo (1932)/1351. ("The Restraining of the Commonalty from the Science of Theology.")

Al-Ghazālī: (*contd.*)

Iqtiṣād = *Al-Iqtiṣād fī-'l-I'tiqād*, Cairo, n.d. (? about 1948). ("The Golden Mean in Belief.") A critical edition, by Drs. I. A. Çubukçu and M. Atay has been published in Ankara in 1962 as *Ankara Üniversitesi Ilāhiyat Fakültesi Yayinlari*, xxxiv.

Maqāṣid = *Maqāsid al-Falāsifa*, Cairo, (1912)/1331. ("The Aims of the Philosophers.")

Maqṣad = *Al-Maqṣad al-Asnā Sharḥ Asmā' Allāh al-Ḥusnā*, Cairo, n.d.

Miḥakk = *K. Miḥakk an-Naẓar fī-'l-Manṭiq*, Cairo, n.d. ("The Touchstone of Thinking.")

Mishkāt = *Mishkāt al-Anwār*, Cairo ("The Niche for Lights"); the figure in brackets refers to the page of the English translation by W. H. T. Gairdner, London, 1924.

Mi'yār = *Mi'yār al-'Ilm*, Cairo. ("The Standard for Knowledge.")

Mīẓān = *Mīẓān al-'Amal*, Cairo (1910)/1328. ("The Criterion of Action.")

Munqidh = *Al-Munqidh min aḍ-Ḍalāl*, Damascus, 1939/1358. ("Deliverance from Error"); this is translated in *Faith and Practice*.

Mustaẓ'hirī, see Goldziher, *Streitschrift*.

Qisṭās = *Al-Qisṭās al-Mustaqīm*, in *Al-Jawāhir al-Ghawālī*, Cairo, 1934/1353. ("The Just Balance.")

Tahāfut = *Tahāfut al-Falāsifa*, ed. M. Bouyges, Beirut, 1927. ("The Inconsistency of the Philosophers.")

Vivification = *Iḥ'ya' 'Ouloûm ed-Dîn ou Vivification des sciences de la foi*, Analyse et Index par G. H. Bousquet, etc. (Paris, 1955)—reference is by paragraphs.

Goldziher (Ignaz):

"Stellung" = "Die Stellung der alten islamischen Orthodoxie zu den antiken Wissenschaften" (*Abhandlungen der königlich preussischen Akademie der Wissenschaften*, 1915, phil.-hist. Kl., no. 8).

Streitschrift = *Streitschrift des Ġaẓālī gegen die Bāṭinijja-Sekte*, Leiden, 1916; abbreviated edition of the *Mustaẓ'hirī*, with commentary.

Hujw. or Hujwīrī =Hujwīrī, *Kashf al-Maḥjūb*, translated by R. A. Nicholson, second edition, London, 1936, etc.

Ibn-al-Athīr =*id.*, *Al-Kāmil fī-t-Ta'rīkh*, Cairo, n.d. (about 1950); a reference to the Hijra year is usually also given.

Integration—see W. Montgomery Watt.

Jabre (Farid):

"Biographie" ="La Biographie et l'œuvre de Ghazali reconsidérées à la lumière des *Ṭabaqāt* de Sobkī". (*Mélanges de l'Institut Dominicain d'Études Orientales du Caire*, i [1954], 73-102.)

Certitude =*La Notion de certitude selon Ghazali*, Paris, 1958.

JRAS =*Journal of the Royal Asiatic Society.*

al-Juwaynī, *Irshād* =*El-Irchad*, ed. and tr. into French by J.-D. Luciani, Paris, 1938 (first reference is to Arabic text). ("Right Guidance.")

Macdonald (Duncan Black), "Life" ="The Life of al-Ghazzālī with special reference to his religious experience and opinions", *Journal of the American Oriental Society*, xx (1899), 71-132.

Massignon (Louis), *Essai* =*Essai sur les origines du lexique technique de la mystique musulmane* (second edition), Paris, 1954.

Passion =*La Passion d'al-Hallaj, martyr mystique de l'Islam* (Paris, 1922).

Niẓām-al-Mulk, *Book of Government* =*The Book of Government or Rules for Kings*, translation of *Siyāset-nāme* by Hubert Darke, London, 1960.

SM =as-Sayyid Murtaḍā, *It'ḥāf as-Sāda*, Cairo (1893)/1311 (a commentary on the *Iḥyā'*).

Smith, M. =Margaret Smith, *Al-Ghazālī the Mystic*, London, 1944.

Subk. =as-Subkī, *Ṭabaqāt ash-Shāfi'iyya al-Kubrā*, Cairo (1906)/1324.

Vivification—see al-Ghazālī.

Watt (W. Montgomery):

"Authenticity" ="The Authenticity of the Works attributed to al-Ghazālī", *JRAS*, 1952, 24-45.

Integration =*Islam and the Integration of Society*, London, 1961.

Watt (W. Montgomery): (*contd.*)
"Political Attitudes" = "Political Attitudes of the Muʿtazilah", *JRAS*, 1963.
"Shīʿism" = "Shīʿism under the Umayyads", *JRAS*, 1960, 158-172.
"Study" = "A Study of al-Ġazālī", *Oriens*, xiii/xiv (1961), 121-131.

ZDMG = *Zeitschrift der deutschen morgenländischen Gesellschaft*.

INDEX

INDEX

(The Arabic article *al-*, with its variants such as *an-*, *ash-*, etc., is neglected in the alphabetical arrangement. An asterisk indicates that bibliographical details are given.)